THE BUSINESS
OF YOGA

Yoga Teaching Guides

As it grows in popularity, teaching yoga requires an increasing set of skills and understanding, in terms of both yoga practice and knowledge. This series of books guides you towards becoming an accomplished, trusted yoga teacher by refining your teaching skills and methods. The series, written by experts in the field, focuses on the key topics for yoga teachers – including sequencing, language in class, anatomy and running a successful and thriving yoga business – and presents practical information in an accessible manner and format for all levels.. Each book is filled with visual aids to enhance the reading experience, and includes 'top tips' to highlight and emphasize key ideas and advice.

in the same series

Qigong in Yoga Teaching and Practice
Understanding Qi and the Use of Meridian Energy
Joo Teoh
ISBN 978 1 78775 652 6
eISBN 978 1 78775 653 3

Supporting Yoga Students with Common Injuries and Conditions
A Handbook for Teachers and Trainees
Dr. Andrew McGonigle
ISBN 978 1 78775 469 0
eISBN 978 1 78775 470 6

Theming Skills for Yoga Teachers
Tools to Inspire Creative and Connected Classes
Tanja Mickwitz
ISBN 978 1 78775 687 8
eISBN 978 1 78775 688 5

Developing a Yoga Home Practice
An Exploration for Yoga Teachers and Trainees
Alison Leighton with Joe Taft
ISBN 978 1 78775 704 2
eISBN 978 1 78775 705 9

Ayurveda in Yoga Teaching
Tarik Dervish and Masha Pimas
ISBN 978 1 78775 595 6
eISBN 978 1 78775 596 3

of related interest

The Online Yoga Teacher's Guide
Get Confident and Thrive Online
Jade Beckett
ISBN 978 1 83997 180 8
eISBN 978 1 83997 181 5

THE BUSINESS OF YOGA

A Guide to Starting, Growing and
Marketing Your Yoga Business

*Katy Appleton
and Natasha Moutran*

SINGING DRAGON
LONDON AND PHILADELPHIA

First published in Great Britain in 2023 by Singing Dragon,
an imprint of Jessica Kingsley Publishers
An imprint of Hodder & Stoughton Ltd
An Hachette Company

1

A CIP catalogue record for this title is available from the
British Library and the Library of Congress

ISBN 978 1 78775 642 7
eISBN 978 1 78775 643 4

Printed and bound by CPI Group (UK) Ltd, Croydon, CR0 4YY

Jessica Kingsley Publishers' policy is to use papers that are natural, renewable and recyclable products and made from wood grown in sustainable forests. The logging and manufacturing processes are expected to conform to the environmental regulations of the country of origin.

Jessica Kingsley Publishers
Carmelite House
50 Victoria Embankment
London EC4Y 0DZ
www.singingdragon.com

CONTENTS

INTRODUCTION

It is from experience that we learn, and Katy and I have undoubtedly learned along the way, having lived and breathed the yoga industry throughout our professional careers. As two yoga teachers who have both built successful businesses over the last two decades, we feel it is time to share our learnings with you through the pages of this book. Our journeys have been different, but we have both committed to this path, following our vision and learning as we go. We've lived the challenges, the break-throughs, the highs and the lows, and consistently stayed the course. We have both stuck at it, which has not always been easy, and continuously done the work on ourselves, sometimes to do with the business side of work, sometimes on our own personal journey.

What we both have is a deep passion for the brilliance of yoga and the incredible transformation it can bring which enriches people's lives. Through its various modalities and the ways it can be shared, there is a greatness that we believe must be spread, and we trust our words and guidance contribute to the sharing of this illuminating practice.

This book will bridge the gap for many between passion and purpose, and building a successful business. Sometimes people can get stuck after a teacher training, or even during their career, and not know how to do some of the foundational elements required to get their business going. This book is intended to help you seamlessly connect and find ways to bring your calling and unique gift to life, and it provides a toolkit for how to brand, market and create a business that serves, in whatever shape or form that is for you.

We have high standards in how we do business, based on what we wish the students' experience to be. This has led us both down the path of authentic service in business, of setting the bar high when it comes to integrity, at all times. We have tripped, flipped, yet owned these along the way, rather than covering them up, and always learned and evolved from our experiences.

The process of writing a book isn't easy, much like running a business – a beautiful reminder in this process of what it can take, and the need for patience, perseverance and dedication. There are parts that are uncomfortable and challenging, yet you learn along the way and can then speak from a place of experience and knowledge, having taken another step further along your path.

This book is an amalgamation of our journeys, learnings, experience and the tools we have found that have helped immensely. It is a collaboration of both of our work and experiences, but for the ease of writing and reading we have one voice. So as you read on, know that the 'I' used is always from the 'We', and the thoughts, wisdom, experience and knowledge from both of us collectively.

As you work your way through this book, some parts will feel more relevant than others. We recommend reading it the whole way through, as there might be useful tips and tools in any section. These could be applied to your business at any stage, or might initiate an insight that can be useful in any context. If you feel the need to skip a chapter that isn't relevant for you right now, go ahead and come back to it when the time is right.

This book is not only something to read and digest, but also to participate in, with a workbook element to it. There are many invitations to do an exercise or take a journalling moment to help you implement the recommendations on offer. We recommend you take your time to read through the chapters and exercises and have a notebook with you to make notes, answer questions or jot down some inspiration.

As you and your business evolve, aspects of what you discover might change, so revisit chapters and redo some of the suggested exercises whenever you feel compelled to. It's fine to continue to adapt and to honour these evolutions when it feels appropriate. Know that this isn't a final process that is set in stone, but a starting place. You can use this throughout your career, as a point of reflection and realignment when necessary.

There is gold in these pages and it is our desire that it lights you up and propels your business to succeed.

Katy and Natasha x

Chapter 1

FIRST STEPS AND ENQUIRY WORK

'Turning a vision into a reality starts with just one small step.'

Welcome to this first step on your yoga teaching journey. Wherever you currently are on your path in this moment, whether you've just completed an accredited yoga teacher training, have been teaching for a while and are looking for a new direction, or are somewhere in between, there are always possibilities for growth, expansion and fresh inspiration that can shift your trajectory. Deciding to evolve in your career really is a choice – a choice to step up and into your truth. In reading this book you have already made a choice to steer your path in a new direction, a direction that I hope will provide you with joy, inspiration, abundance and the feeling of true fulfilment in your career, and ultimately in life. So, thank you for taking that step towards your evolution.

I believe that we are all truly here for a purpose, that each of us has something so unique and wonderful to offer, and that often it is our life's work to find out what that is. Once we do, then the work is to realize it and take the steps to live it, breathe it and share it with the world. You are absolutely the right person to do whatever it is that you were born to do. You have the talents and gifts for that, and now it is time to get the tools in place, to gain clarity and focus on how to begin the journey of stepping into it, teaching, sharing and being the light you are meant to be. You already know deep down that you're here to share and teach from this space of inner wisdom, and that's what most likely led you to doing a yoga teacher training in the first place.

Starting out on a new career path can often be daunting. Perhaps some doubts, fears and even uncertainties can creep in. Our self-doubt, limiting beliefs and more can have a field day when we decide to take the brave step of starting something new and making a change. This is completely normal and, trust me, we've all been there; however, in those moments it is important to remember that you are on this path for an absolute reason, and that only you will do it the way you do it. That is *why* you're doing it. Something deep within you already knows that. There may be many yoga teachers out there in the world, but only you will teach the way you teach, and that is your signature and what will allow you to carve out your own career path and attract your ideal students and dream clients to you.

So, let's begin with you, as *you* and *your* soul are the core essence and root from which all of this can grow – your work, your brand and more. *You* are *totally unique* and that is your power. Not one single person on this planet has had the same life journey as you, the same upbringing, the same experiences, the same education, the same training that you have had, in the way in which you have absorbed them, lived them, processed them and can share them with the world. That in itself makes you distinctive, and it is that quality that will help mould you into the teacher or practitioner you will become, that you already are in fact. So, before you begin designing your future and laying down the path to get there, let's look at where you are right now, your journey so far and what you already have.

Reflection exercise

This is a beautiful practice of self-reflection and gratitude that will take up to 30 minutes.

I find that looking back, taking a moment of reflection and gratitude, can often help us process where we have been, realize where we are and allow us to consciously move forwards. Taking a moment to be present and assess the 'journey' so far is a vital part of our journey and evolution. This practice is not so much about taking us back into our past stories, but to help us realize the importance of using our past to learn and grow, and ultimately assist us in stepping into our next chapter.

For this practice, you will need a quiet space and a journal. I recommend reading through the whole practice first before you begin, so you can be more present while you're in the process.

THE PRACTICE

Meditation and contemplation

- Take a moment to sit in stillness.

- Carve out some time for this in a quiet space.

- Sit comfortably with a notebook.

- Close your eyes, take five minutes to connect to your breath and your body.

- If you have a meditation practice, you may choose to do a short meditation or a pranayama practice.

- Take at least ten minutes to become present and begin to consider your journey so far in this lifetime that will have led you to this moment as a yoga teacher.

- Sit with whatever comes up as you look at your personal journey into this world of yoga so far. Anything that arises, small or big, is perfect.

- You may choose to look at influences you've had, what first brought you to your mat and how your practice has evolved.

- Consider what contributed to you becoming a yoga teacher and stepping into the role.

- Now go beyond your yoga practice. What are your other influences or inspirations? Maybe other spiritual practices, teachers, a friend who took you to your first yoga class or your parents?

- Consider the relationships you've had and how they've played a part in bringing you to this path.

- Whatever it is, whatever comes, let it.

Journalling

- Allow for whatever comes naturally to arise, to flow through you, and, when you feel ready, begin to write it all down. Take at least ten minutes to write what comes to you.

- Write freely and unedited, just a pouring of consciousness onto the page.

- This practice is like a short yogi autobiography. Enjoy this reflection with no expectation and allow any emotions to arise. Take all the time you need.

- It doesn't have to be in chronological order, just continue to ask the question and let what comes come. Trust the flow completely.

- Know that whatever comes to mind will be for a reason; trust what arises, even if it may not seem obvious or relevant.

Reflection

- Write all you need to and then take a quiet moment to read it all back.

- You may want to read it out loud to yourself or to someone close to you.

- This is your journey so far that has led you to this moment. Take a moment of gratitude for all of these moments, people, events, both positive and challenging, as they have led you here and played a role in your journey.

- Once this has been completed, notice what you have learned from these experiences. What insights and reflections revealed themselves to you?

- Consider what they gave you and how they helped get you to where you are now.

- Consider the main things that have jumped out at you and what this could be telling you about yourself, about your journey so far and where it is pointing to, what it is leading you towards, and perhaps what your life purpose could be.

- What have you learned along the way that others could benefit from?

- Take some time to close your practice, in whatever way feels appropriate for you.

So, what is next?

This is the question I remember asking myself after I completed my first yoga teacher training. I had gone through a huge transformational journey, months of learning and discovering, my eyes being opened to a whole new world, as well as making the decision that this was the path I was meant to be on. But then, I remember on the day I received my certificate being caught off guard with this question...so what now? And I know I'm not the only one. Whether it be straight after our first training, early on in our career or even at times well into our career, maybe after completing a new milestone, this question can still pop up and stir us.

The conscious career path

There are a few ways in which we can navigate ourselves from this space of enquiry and we'll be touching on two main viewpoints to help give it perspective:

- *The big picture:* our big-sky view, dreams, the life vision, the goals, the purpose.

- *The current reality:* where you stand right now, and the reality of what is possible in your current world and situation.

In order to create a clear road map of your A–Z, A being your *current reality* and Z being your *big picture* in your conscious career path, first you must be realistic about your starting place, as well as gain a clear understanding on what it is that you wish to be navigating towards. And, of course, this may change over time and that is totally fine and natural. So, let's get some clarity here.

JOURNALLING MOMENT

Ask yourself the following questions to reveal your current reality:

- What qualifications and certifications do I have? What have I studied?

- What do these enable me to do exactly? (What am I trained to do and what can I be insured to do?)

- What do I feel confident offering/teaching/sharing/holding space for?

- Where do I still need to grow/learn/develop? Do I feel inspired to share these aspects?

- What experiences and skills do I have?

Based on your answers, consider if you are right now, at this moment, ready to move into the path you feel called to.

- Do you already feel confident and inspired to share your wisdom with others?

- Do you feel you can offer this work with clarity, confidence and authenticity?

If so, then perfect. You are in exactly the right place you need to be to take the next steps. If perhaps you're not sure, or you feel deep down that you're not there yet, that's okay too. Being in tune and honest with where you are is vital. If you jump in too soon, a few things could potentially happen. You may end up facing some challenges, perhaps not making a great first impression, burning yourself out, feeling as if you're meeting resistance whenever you try to move forwards, or even just losing momentum. In most cases, it won't work. It may, of course, end up working out just fine and you'll find your way through and learn as you go. This doesn't mean you shouldn't move forwards at all; it is about owning where you are and *what* the next steps should be in a logical, grounded and intelligent way. However, be conscious of any limiting beliefs that might be arising telling you that you're not ready yet, when actually you absolutely are, and you have everything you already need in order to proceed.

The career vinyasa

Just as you would approach planning and sequencing a yoga class, there are steps to take. In the same way that you most likely warm up the body and prepare for certain bigger poses, your career follows a similar pattern. It's a vinyasa – carefully thought-out steps made when the time is right and you feel ready for them, with all your heart and wisdom, and with authenticity and integrity. Some people can jump and really land on their feet, and potentially that may work. But often, for real longevity, it is better to take the time to prepare well and go step by step.

It is often said by teachers, mentors and many successful people in all industries, that careful preparation is the key to success and feeling a sense of ease around your work.

DON'T QUITE FEEL READY YET? WHAT IS THE NEXT STEP?

More studying

- What areas do you need more knowledge on?
- Who or where would you like to study?

Practice, practice, practice

- Do you need to gain more teaching experience?
- Building confidence teaching free or discounted classes?

Further support

- Assisting your teacher to deepen your learning
- Get a mentor who can support your growth

These are all steps you can take towards your purpose, while still carving out a plan along the way, but remaining true to what you are ready for.

The vision

Now let's take a look at the big sky view, the dream, *the bigger picture.*

Before embarking on this journey, you will need to be crystal clear on what you *really* want and to be honest about where you're at currently. This is *not* about putting roadblocks in your way, but about looking down the road ahead and assessing the potential road bumps you may come up against before you reach them. When we set a pinpoint for our compass of life, work, or whatever it is, we don't always have a clear path to that place. That is not only okay, but to be expected. It is part of our journey, our growth and our learning. I don't think you'll find a single person who is flourishing in their career or has made a real impact in this world, however big or small, who didn't come across some challenges along the way. These are the growth edges and often the biggest learnings. I like to think of them as growing pains, our own career growing pains. When the end point is clear, when the overall intention is set, then these bumps, these growing pains can be handled with more ease. We can begin to navigate our way through, because we understand the overall purpose and intention behind what it is that we are doing. Hence why it's so important to take time over this stage. The intention and purpose behind what we do allows us to make decisions more easily, to shift and change when we have to and to keep bringing ourselves back on track in those moments when perhaps we get a little knocked off course.

The yoga world has beautifully expanded in recent years. In just the last few years alone the industry has seen a dramatic increase in yoga teacher trainings, with more and more people qualifying and deepening their practice and studies. It is a blessing for humanity really. I am often asked how I feel about so many teacher trainings out there, with a sense that some feel as if completing a yoga teacher training is the new 'thing to do', a trend perhaps. I can hand on heart say that the more yoga there is in the world the better, and so I will only ever choose to see this as an elevation for society. The more consciously connected and present human being are, the better for our planet and society.

However, it is important to note that, in my opinion, not all teacher trainings are held to the same quality standards of training, education and due diligence as others. I say this with absolute love, and yet from experience of seeing, time and time again, teachers who have completed a training and walked away not feeling that they have gained the skills, education or experience to hold the seat of a teacher with absolute confidence, safety and integrity.

The longer I work, teach, live and embody this practice, the more respect I have for it and the endless capacity it has for creating transformation within. And this ability must be honoured, respected and handled with care.

The why

I believe the best starting place for any project or venture is with the *why*.

Why is it you want to do what you are setting out to do? Why do you feel called to share this service? Why does it need to exist and why are *you* driven to doing it?

JOURNALLING MOMENT

Take some time to journal or consider:

- What is fuelling the passion behind what you want to achieve?

- What is your purpose? There is usually a deep need within us, a calling in our souls, that asks us to step onto a certain path or pursue a particular career in this lifetime.

- What sets you alight?

- What stirs your soul?

We each carry a set of 'tools' with us that can be utilized and called on as a teacher. Our toolbox may include our actual teaching training skills, but also a host of other skillsets. We each carry a unique collection of techniques, qualities and attributes that can already contribute to our path.

Look not only at your experiences, training and life moments that led you to where you are and contribute to what you have to offer, but also at your strengths. What qualities do you have that will help you along this journey?

All of these elements are the makings of what makes you *you*. Whether you have just become a teacher or practitioner, or already are one and are looking to expand and grow in your teaching journey, you are in essence moving to a place of not only holding space, but sharing your learnings, qualities, talents and experiences with others. In doing so, you become an amplified version of yourself. You are stepping into a space of opening a part of yourself up for others to see. Of course, this can be done on a very small scale and with strong professional boundaries, but the truth is, what will make you stand out from another teacher, or what will draw a student to you specifically as opposed to someone else is...well...*you*.

Therefore, it is imperative that in order to project yourself further down your chosen career path, to step into your career in a bigger capacity, you need to go inwards also, and develop a deeper understanding of *who* you are, *what* it is that you really have to offer, *why* you want to offer this, *what* your purpose is and *who* will benefit from it.

Finding, or even just thinking about, your life purpose for many is not always a quick and easy job, but perhaps the uncovering and exploration of this in itself will become part of what you offer and the place from which you can share from. It is all valuable, and there is a beauty in trusting the timing of life unfolding. It may change as you go, and that is perfect also. It is up to you to put the work in. One thing I have learned, over and over again, is that many of life's opportunities won't come knocking on your door, but you can absolutely go knocking on a few doors to seek out life's opportunities. The 'work' is being aligned with your own truth allowing this abundance to flow into your life with ease.

Take a moment to write down your mission statement as explained in the images below. A mission statement is a written declaration of your purpose, your heart-orientated values and the core of what drives you forward in this lifetime. It is said that we all come here with a 'mission' and connecting to this and writing it out clearly is a powerful tool. It is the *why* behind all that you do. It may just be a short sentence or few sentences that simply summarize what it is that is calling you to do what you do.

YOUR MISSION STATEMENT

Your mission statement is a message of your heart's desire and calling through the work that you choose to do.

This doesn't have to be long or complicated.

Let it come from within and flow from a space of connection to your truth.

Take some time to sit quietly.

Connect inwards in the way that feels appropriate for you right now.
Slow down the thoughts and drop into your heart space so that you can write from this deeper space and connect to your inner knowing.

You may wish to use some of these questions as a prompt to journal from:

What are you passionate about?
What are you called to do?
What inspires you?
What humanitarian causes speak to you?
Where do you feel called to speak up and make a difference?
What are your deepest desires in this lifetime?
What do you wish for your legacy to be?

MY MISSION STATEMENT

Once you have your mission statement written, or perhaps this is a piece of writing in progress, then you can consider how it will begin to manifest itself tangibly in your world.

What does this look like practically in your life and how can you action this through what you do?

What do you choose to create in this world and what do you share?

From what you've written, you may start to notice a theme, feeling or even very clear calling emerging. It may be super obvious who you want to work with, the kinds of offerings you want to put out there and so on, or it may still be something you need to sit and feel into. If so, give it space and time. As you begin to teach you'll start to notice what flows with ease and where you may feel more resistance.

Listen to that and trust it, noticing what flows and, if resistance is there, why?

JOURNALLING MOMENT

If you have clarity around this, then you can start to think about and write about who you see yourself teaching:

- What are the groups, types of people and communities?

- Where do you see yourself teaching?

- What do you think will be your main draw?

As you begin to explore more deeply who you are as a teacher, another valuable reflection is to consider what your strengths are. Sometimes we can be quite unaware of the qualities we exude or the impact we have on others – the feeling they are left with after being around us or what they gain from our presence, classes, teachings, offerings or even just from the people we are.

YOUR QUALITIES

What do you consider to be your top 5 qualities?

Write them down and be generous with yourself.

YOUR QUALITIES

Now write down what you consider to be your top five qualities are as a teacher and in your business

HOW OTHERS SEE YOU

Finally, a beautiful practice I highly recommend, is asking friends, family, clients, what they see as the **top 3–5 qualities** they admire most about you.

Ask them to be honest, and try to be open to receiving their admiration and feedback.

Let yourself receive their words with grace and absorb into your heart as you accept and acknowledge what they wish to share with you.

Ask your peers, colleagues and friends from your teacher training what qualities they saw shine through you during your training or when you're teaching?

This can really say a lot about the kind of teacher we are and what people might be drawn to us for and therefore what we might be best focusing on.

It can sometimes be a surprise and qualities we didn't even know we embodied start to come through that you may choose to embrace and develop as you get more clarity on your direction and purpose.

WHAT OTHERS SHARED ABOUT
MY TOP QUALITIES AND GIFTS

Chapter 2

NEW BEGINNINGS

'You are here for a purpose…the fun is in finding out what that is.'

This chapter is speaking predominantly to newly qualified teachers, although there are aspects that can absolutely be applied to anyone even if you've been teaching for a while and maybe want to explore new work opportunities or expand your business.

When starting out on your teaching journey, as mentioned already, there are many avenues you could go down. The options are endless, depending on the types of classes you want to offer, the groups you wish to work with and so on. For some of you, it will be super clear and for others it may not be so obvious just yet, and that's okay. The most important thing is just to get out there and get teaching.

When you have just qualified, you are going into the teaching realm with your 'L' plates on. In reality, this is where much of the real growth and evolution happens, and everything you have learned, experienced and absorbed during your studies has time to really assimilate and be digested, as well as put into practice. It is only once you start actively teaching students that the real learning happens. As much as you can pre-empt scenarios, situations, students, bodies and so on, you will never really know how to step into the role of holding space as a teacher until you have real-life students in front of you and you are called to step up.

These early days are essential and amazing in that way. They allow for the real understanding and embodiment of everything you have learned to be revealed on a deeper level. You may also find that as you teach, you learn more about yourself and who you are as a teacher – your teaching style, what you're really good at and maybe the areas in which you still need to grow. You might find out more about what inspires you, what you feel more called to share or focus on, and even the types of people who are called to work with you. All of this is telling and a great insight that can help guide you moving forwards.

A few recommendations for new teachers

Transparency

As a new teacher, it can be tempting to feel the need to 'prove' yourself perhaps in some way. In my humble opinion, being honest, open and transparent with where you are in your journey will not only serve you well but is often actually received in a very positive light.

Don't underestimate your training, your experience and what you have to offer already. And equally, be wary of trying to step into a space you're maybe not quite ready for. Be honest with where you are, both with yourself and your employers, clients or students. This won't make them think you are less capable and if anything may simply let them offer you some grace as you learn your craft. This also gives you permission to make mistakes, so you can relax somewhat in knowing you have already set realistic expectations. It is okay to say you are just starting out, and it is absolutely okay to admit when you are not sure of something rather than just fake it.

Feedback

As you are starting out, I would encourage you to ask for feedback whenever possible. I know this can be daunting at times, but if we can reframe it as helpful feedback and growth opportunities then it can be invited in and received with love. When we're new to something and potentially still make mistakes and are trying to build confidence, then asking for feedback can really take us into our vulnerability.

However, more than likely, you'll be amazed at how positive and encouraging the feedback is. This is your opportunity to learn and evolve.

Every bit of feedback really is a gift and can be taken in a positive way, even when it may feel negative at the time, as it is inviting you to look at something, change something or become aware of something. It lets you step up and challenge yourself to be even better.

This is helpful to do at the beginning to get out of any bad habits from the get go, to build confidence as you take on all the lovely feedback, and to begin to discern where your strengths are as a teacher and what people like you and your classes for. It may even give you some content you could use for future marketing and prompting.

Of course, this isn't limited to new teachers or something that you should do just at the beginning of your journey, and actually it is a good habit to get into throughout your career as it is so valuable to know what your students and clients are feeling. It enables you to adapt and change as you go, based on their feedback. These insights can really help you navigate your way through your career. They will help you grow, learn, evolve and adapt when it's time to.

Getting work

As a rule of thumb when you're starting out it is recommended to get teaching as and where you can. At the start, you really just want to gain experience and get using your skills, so taking on cover work and anything that is offered, within reason, is probably a good starting place. As long as you feel ready and qualified to take something on, and it interests you and excites you, then say yes to opportunities as you'll learn from every one of them, even if they don't perhaps quite align with the bigger vision just yet.

Approaching studios

Go in, go to class, chat to the front of house or managers, chat to your teachers, let them know you have qualifications, what your positive qualities are and what you're passionate about sharing. Then be bold enough to put yourself out there and ask about potential work opportunities or cover lists. You might need to audition to get on a cover list, so be ready for that and have a class plan handy and well prepared and practised for when the opportunity arises. Having a class you know back to front and inside out will really allow you to shine and show off your skills and personality as a teacher. Know your class plan well enough that if something goes wrong or distracts you, you won't be thrown off and can stay in your power and hold the space in the seat of the teacher, as well as ease into being in flow and being natural. If you do get asked to cover a class at the last minute, take the chance, be prepared, ask the teacher or someone at the studio what is normally expected, the level of students, the vibe and so on, so you can really know what to offer and then go for it and *enjoy it*. Don't worry about trying to be similar to the teacher you're covering, instead be the best you can be and let yourself shine doing what you do, know and love. Your authenticity and passion will speak louder than your desire to impress or even to impersonate another great teacher.

Does it align with you?

When you get an 'in' at a studio, whether it's for cover work or something more permanent, ask yourself if it feels like a right fit for you. It can be very flattering and tempting for many reasons to jump at offers, but if it doesn't resonate with you then it may not be conducive. As we know, there are *many* styles of yoga out there, many approaches, intentions, vibes and even each studio may have a different ethos behind it, its own business model and the type of people it caters for and so on. Be sure to get to know the studio you want to teach at, and get a feel for what it is all about. What does it stand for, who runs it, what are their values and mission statement and does it align with your own? This is not to say that any one viewpoint on teaching is right or wrong, it's simply about finding the right fit for both sides and staying aligned to your truth and your integrity.

Of course, you may choose to take on work opportunities not so aligned if needed; however, you may find that eventually, if it's not matched up with the reasons you are choosing to teach, then eventually this will show in one way or another. Doing something that isn't in alignment with our true path can often deplete us, leave us feeling unfulfilled. Often the universe has a way of ending it anyway, until we learn the lesson to stay on track with our path.

I share this from much personal experience, having learned this lesson many times the hard way. When I started teaching yoga I was offered some amazing teaching gigs at some reputable studios. The classes were big, the studios were well known and it was a great boost and step in my teaching path to be able to teach in these places. Of course, I said yes for many reasons and at first really thrived and enjoyed these classes and loved the students. But slowly, something started to not feel quite right. I realized I was adapting my authentic teaching style quite a lot, to align with the studio owners, the studio ethos or the wants of the students. Sadly, this was to the detriment of my own personal values and at times my own integrity as a teacher. With no judgement of other teachers' ways, studios and practitioners, there really is a place for everyone, but there came a point that I realized I wasn't following my own personal beliefs as a teacher. I was no longer honouring what I felt I wanted to teach and share and the way in which I wanted to help people transform. It also wasn't what naturally wanted to flow from me, so after a while it just started to feel a bit forced, and I got burnt out. When I was being asked to do things that didn't necessarily sit right with me and the way in which I felt comfortable holding space, then I knew it was time to walk away and reassess where and who I should be teaching. It was such a valuable lesson and I am so grateful for those times, those studios for giving me the opportunity, the students for trusting me and ultimately eventually being able to learn from it and see that my own journey was maybe in a different direction. Taking a step back from these experiences, and not seeing them as setbacks in any way, but instead a beautiful redirection back onto the path I was meant to be on, allowed me to continuously re-evaluate and eventually find my flow and purpose.

If your aim is to start working in a different capacity than in studios, perhaps in corporate yoga or starting your own classes, then a lot of the above is still relevant.

JOURNALLING MOMENT

Consider the following things:

- What do you want to offer?

- Where do you want to be teaching?

- Who would benefit from your teaching?

- What commitment would you like to make?

We will go into this in more depth later in the book but for now begin to think about these things and where you can start to practise, test the waters and get some trial classes going. Put feelers out and maybe think about offering some free classes to see what the response is like, if you enjoy it, if there is a demand for what you're wanting to do and for feedback. Whatever it is, get going and just start. Even if you're not yet sure exactly where you're going, most likely once you begin teaching you'll soon get a better feel for what you do and don't enjoy and what resonates with you. Trust the process!

Chapter 3

YOUR BRAND

'Let your brand be the highest version of yourself.'

As a yoga teacher, or any freelancer for that matter, your brand essentially is *you*. Developing your brand therefore could seem like an easy task – after all, who knows you better than yourself? However, I've noticed that for many people this is not always the most natural thing to do. In fact, sometimes making a brand out of yourself and what you offer, instead of something external to you, can be even more challenging. The ability to 'sell' ourselves is not the most natural thing for many of us, especially when we are following our calling and are being driven more by our bigger purpose than financial gain. But that does not mean it isn't possible and often it simply needs a little shift in perspective and some helpful tools to get there. Creating your brand from an aligned conscious space is absolutely achievable, and will most likely also generate the best outcome in your business or work.

This chapter will keep things simple and offer ways for you to build the foundations for your business and start to develop your brand easily and effectively. If it is helpful at times to remove yourself from it a little and look at it as a separate entity from you, then do that. Sometimes shifting the perspective can help us gain clarity. For the purpose of development, allow yourself the freedom to look at it from different angles at times – the sky view. Sometimes from your centred self, sometimes removed from it looking in at it as if it were its own being, sometimes from the perspective of your ideal client. When you feel that you are honouring all of these aspects and speaking to all of these perspectives at once, then you know you are on the right track.

I invite you to put yourself in the seat of your student or client as regularly as possible. They are, after all, the person you are speaking to and calling in, so changing the focus from you and what you want to say or share, to them and what they want and need will be extremely beneficial throughout this process. As you are on the path of being of service, this is generally good practice anyway, and so as you would when holding space or teaching, come back to them and their needs when looking at what it is you want to share and how. Your business is a reflection of your teaching and vice versa, so practising the same principles you would use when teaching is always advised.

Branding is how you present, promote or showcase your business, product or service to the world. In this case, the business is you and your offerings as a teacher. Up to this point, we have focused on getting clarity on who you are as a teacher, your identity as a yoga teacher and your mission statement. These will all directly influence the development of your brand. This next phase is focused on the *how*. How can you take everything you have been considering and working on and package it up in a way that not only portrays the right message of who you are, what you stand for and what you offer, but also attracts the right people to you. I find this bit great fun, but I understand that for many at first it can be overwhelming. If the thought of creating your brand is daunting at all, try and look at this as an exciting creative process that can be enjoyable and inspiring to work through.

Your brand will be your identity in the yoga world. This includes the 'look and feel' of everything you 'show' to the world, from your logo, your website and your business cards all the way to your tone of voice in any communication with your clients and on social media and promotional materials. After all, it is your brand that is your 'packaging', and therefore it needs to express all that you are and offer in a way that is as aligned as possible with your essence and your mission statement. You may also want to consider your brand message or story. This is the conversation around your brand and what it stands for and represents in this world. This may be about yoga, but it may be about something bigger than that on a humanitarian level, which you then put into practice through sharing yoga.

Brand feel

A beautiful way to start this process is to consider what lasting effect and impact you wish to have on your students after working with them.

JOURNALLING MOMENT

Consider these few questions:

- When a student leaves your class, how do you want them to feel?

- What kind of things would you want them to say about you and your teaching?

- What would they get from your class that has a positive influence on their life?

- What is the impact and impression you want to make?

Here is a little exercise that can help you tap in and connect to this a little more easily. For this exercise, you will need a quiet space for at least 15 minutes and your journal.

EXERCISE

Meditation and contemplation

- Take a moment to sit quietly.

- Maybe put on some music that inspires you or that you might play in your classes.

- Create an ambiance that helps provoke the feelings and setting you would want to create in your business.

- Take five minutes to breathe and sit in meditation.

- Allow your body to settle, your breath to extend, and then slow down and relax.

- Maybe even move your body a little if that feels inviting.

- Begin to quieten the mind and bring your awareness into your physical body.

- As you ground and settle, begin to think about your work.

- Think over your mission statement, what it is that you are called to share with the world

- Now visualize your business, your work, your classes, your students, whatever comes to mind.

Journalling

- Take time to consider this and write down everything that comes to you.

- It might just be words, it could be sentences, all is perfect, just allow yourself to express the desire you hold for how people would feel after you share your offerings with them.

- Notice what it feels like in your body.

- What emotions and feelings do you want to invoke in them?

- What qualities do you wish to awaken in them?

- What values do you feel are being embodied through your work?

Reflection

- These qualities are the essence of your brand. Sit with this feeling and your words for a moment.

This is your brand 'personality' and how it will be seen by the world. Everything you develop, from your website, to a flyer, even to an email or personal exchange with a student, can come from this place and this core identity.

Consider, how you can recreate these feelings, emotions and qualities in every aspect of your business.

You can use this list as a foundation for so many aspects of your business moving forwards, and refer to it as often as you need to.

Yogi avatar

When we talk about branding and about communicating with your client, it is vital to know who exactly your client is. In order to do this, we can create something called a client avatar, or a yogi avatar as I like to call it. This is a very specific description of your dream student or client. It might be an actual person you know that you are really tailoring your business to as an example, or it may be the ideal person you'd love to share your offerings with and are calling in.

This will align, of course, with your mission statement, so it may be worth giving that a read or having it next to you as you go through this process. Keep checking that you are on track with your higher purpose of what you are doing through your work, and who it is that you wish to teach and share this with.

If your business is oriented more towards other businesses, companies or groups for corporate yoga, for example, then perhaps consider one person who might be within that 'group' and describe them.

Of course, there will always be a variety of people with whom we want to work, and it is important to keep that flexibility and not alienate a potential student, but getting very specific and being more niche can be very helpful. This is really on a case-by-case basis and so I encourage you to sit with that and honour what feels true to you always.

For the following exercise, you'll need at least 20 minutes to sit quietly with your journal.

EXERCISE FOR CREATING YOUR DREAM CLIENT – YOUR YOGI AVATAR

Meditation

- Find a comfortable seat and take a moment to connect inwards.

- Close your eyes and relax your body.

- Focus on your breath and let it start to lengthen and slow down.

- Take as long as you need here to feel yourself come into a space of meditation or contemplation.

- Empty your mind and let your thoughts slow down.

- Keep coming back to your breath and this present moment.

Visualization

- Once you feel centred in your being, spend some time visualizing your dream client.

- Sit and picture your absolute dream client – the one who will benefit from what it is that you have to offer, who will be called to it, who needs it, who will be able to experience actual transformation through your work.

- Picture them as vividly as possible:

  - What do they look like?

  - How old are they?

  - Where do they live?

  - What do they enjoy doing?

  - How do they dress?

  - Where do they spend their time and who do they spend it with?

- Do they work and if so what do they do?

- What sparks joy in their world?

- What are their fears?

- What problems, challenges or issues may they be facing in life?

- Where in their life do they need more support and how can you offer this to them?

- What do they really need that they may not even know themselves yet?

Journalling and mood board

- Spend time creating as full a picture as you can and write down everything that comes to mind.

- It doesn't matter how broad or specific the details are, just let yourself visualize this person as specifically as possible.

- If you wish, make a mood board or vision board of this.

Connecting with your dream client

As you picture this person, you may also want to ask them in your mind:

- What would you enjoy the most from what it is I have to offer?

- How can I be of service to you?

- What can I share with you?

- What have I learned so far on my journey that you will benefit from knowing?

- How would you like me to communicate with you?

- What 'issue or challenge' are you facing in life that I can help with? Write down whatever comes to mind.

Reflection

- Take a moment to read back over your notes and reflect on what came up for you and how this makes you feel.

This can be a really powerful tool to use not only when creating your brand, but also in regard to anything to do with your business. It is something I will refer back to throughout this book when it comes to other tools for building your business, such as marketing strategies, social media, pricing and so forth, as ultimately everything you create and offer is designed with this person in mind. It can therefore be useful to use this as the foundation for many decisions moving forwards and to help the general trajectory of your work. Of course, it's important to note that this can change and be edited or adjusted at any time if it begins to not feel relevant or accurate or to resonate anymore. It is encouraged, actually, to stay true to your heart and purpose always. So, if this begins to change and adapt over time, which is inevitable to some extent as we change and grow as human beings, then your business, students and clients will most likely mirror this shift. Your core purpose, if felt deeply as your life purpose, will probably stay the same in its purest essence, but the way in which it manifests in life and the people you choose to work with may change over time so be comfortable adapting and changing with that natural progression.

Now that you have an idea of your avatar created in your mind and on paper you can begin to tailor your brand, and, in the next chapters, your marketing and social media specifically towards them.

Brand development

The beauty of clever branding is finding a way to allow everyone who comes into contact with your brand to feel the exact qualities and characteristics you just wrote down, to feel the essence of it shine through.

For example, if the qualities that you would like your students to feel are 'alive, energized, and creative' when they've been with you or in your class, then you want to make sure these are the exact qualities that exude from every aspect of your business through your branding, design, communication and brand story.

Take some time to consider your list and what makes you feel these things. What colours, shapes, textures and elements connect you to this or resonate with this?

Pull together any colours, images, photos and so on that inspire you and give you the same felt sense of what it is you want to create. You can make this a fun, creative process, finding a way that excites you and choosing whatever form inspires you the most. If you are a visual person, maybe try putting together a mood board or an online vision board. Start to notice what you are drawn to in life.

What colours, elements, images, words and places really resonate for you as well as connect with your mission statement and the essence you want to create.

Begin to take note of the brands that really speak to you, be they in the yoga world or not. Take note of what it is about them that resonates with you, that speaks to a part of you and get curious as to how that may be happening. Is it through their use of language? Is it the vibe, images, the creative design they use? What else could it be? See what draws your eye and begin to make notes of this. You can begin to pull everything together as you create your own Brand Book. I like to use an online document so I can add bits as I go, change and shift things around, include images, quotes and colours I like and so on, gradually building and editing it as I get more clarity on what resonates with the business.

Logo

When designing your logo, there are several things you can consider and options to choose from, depending on style, preference and budget.

- **Hire a designer to create a logo for you:** This is a good option if you have a start-up budget in place to begin your business. If you do go this route I recommend asking around, looking at a few different people, seeing previous work to make sure it resonates with you and that you like their style. Get a quote, making sure you have clarity on exactly what this includes, such as how many amendments you can make and so on and what the deliverables are. You can then share your vision with them, the Brand Book if you have created one, or simply explain your ideas for the look and feel, see what they come back with and take it from there. The clearer you are on what you want, the more a designer will be able to really create something unique and perfect for you and your business so be mindful to not rush into this step before you're ready.

- **Do a skills exchange with a designer:** This is a brilliant option and one I have used and recommend to anyone who doesn't have much of a budget to start with. In this scenario you can ask friends, friends of friends, people on social media and so on, for anyone who is maybe starting out as a designer and would be open to an exchange, or perhaps a student who wants to gain experience. The process can be similar to the above. I would recommend in any situation where you choose to do an exchange, for example having a logo created in exchange for the designer attending some yoga classes, that you are very clear on what is expected from the beginning and make sure you both feel that the time and energy involved in this trade is fair.

- **Create a logo yourself:** If you are creative in that way and have a clear vision then why not go for it and create your own personal logo? There are many websites and software programmes that can help you generate this easily.

- **Keep it simple:** There is absolutely nothing wrong with having a super simple logo. This could just be the name in a nice font of some sort. Often this is enough and if you wish to keep your look and feel more simple, subtle and modern then this can be a really lovely way of achieving that with no budget needed, and it can be done very quickly.

Overall design elements

This covers the overall look and feel in anything other than the logo. For example, your newsletter, social media, flyers, business cards and so on. As mentioned previously, if you have a budget you may choose to hire a designer to help with all of this. If not, it is totally possible to have a cohesive brand style throughout your business. Here are some things to consider:

- **Typography:** It can be helpful to pick two or three fonts that work well with your logo, your 'vibe', that you use throughout your business, that match your brand look and your logo and also work well together, complementing each other. If you search on the internet you can often find a 'theme' of a few different fonts that have been grouped together to work nicely for any materials. It can be nice to stick to these on your website and promotional materials, to add a feeling of cohesion and so people will become familiar with your 'look'.

- **Colour palette:** This is a vital part of your brand and can quite quickly connect someone to your brand. People will get used to your branding and look and feel, and once they do it can be a very beautiful marketing tool. How wonderful if someone sees a post of yours, for example, and straightaway knows it's you before they even see your name, just because they know your brand identity and associate with it already. People like consistency and it is pleasing to the eye and the soul. So take some time to create a colour palette that suits your brand identity and personality. What colors do you like, would draw in the eye of your ideal client and would invoke the general emotion you're trying to create?

- **Textures:** This can be one that is easily forgotten, but I'm a big fan of considering texture when it comes to branding. What textures, feel and elements connect with your brand? For example, is it sleek, shiny, slick? Or more natural textures with grainy feels, swirls and shapes that mirror what would be found in nature itself? Do you want a bright, sharp, glossy image, or a subtle, textured, one-colour backdrop? This could be used in anything from the background of your website, newsletter or flyers, to the actual tangible materials you might use, such as the type of paper for business cards, the props you buy and so on, depending on how far you wish to take it.

- **Images:** Use of images is of course a huge aspect of your branding, even more so now with social media such a huge aspect of promoting a business. As with the elements already mentioned, a cohesive look to images and photos used can really help you stay aligned to the look and feel of the business. This might even be a starting point for creating the look you'd like to achieve in a photoshoot if that is something you would consider in order to get content for your website, social media, marketing and so on. It can also simply be the style of images you use throughout your branding, even if it's not you personally or from your own photoshoot.

  Have a think about the look and feel, tone, colours and vibe that would fit with your brand. Who do you want these images to jump out to? What do you want them to say about you and your business? What part of you do you want to express in them? This can be down to anything from colours, what you're wearing, environment, editing, filters used and more. I highly recommend finding a style that feels authentic to you and aligned with your brand vision and then keeping that thread going throughout.

- **Language:** The tone of voice and language you use for your business is also a part of your brand and the way in which you communicate what you do with your yogi avatar or ideal client. This will come in more later when we get to writing copy for your website and marketing; however, it can be a good starting place to consider the tone you use to communicate with your clients already. What kind of language do you use to describe what you do? What tone of voice would most grab your ideal client's attention? Is it relaxed and chatty? Friendly and personal? Strong, bold and provocative? How would your dream client best receive what you do and want to be communicated to? This can just be a few words or maybe whole passages come to you. Let it flow and feel natural. It's important this resonates as you will always be creating new content and writing copy, so make sure this tone can flow through you with ease, clarity and integrity.

Carve out some time to consider the above points and enjoy the process. Be playful and creative and let it flow naturally. If you find yourself getting stuck at all, don't forget to look around you. Get out in nature, do your practice, mediate or chat to those who know you best and see what flows. Look through other brands that speak to you, notice what images jump out at you and maybe even start to write in a journal or make a note of what is being shown to you as a starting place. Whatever you do, don't force it. Creativity doesn't flow easily under pressure.

Chapter 4

MARKETING AND PROMOTING

'The way you make people feel will be your legacy.'

Marketing is fundamentally the bridge between you (your business, brand, service or product) and your clients or students. It is the way in which you will communicate with your clients and reach your ideal market, and therefore an absolute necessity to building and growing a sustainable yoga business. No matter the scale of your business, or what you wish for it to be, you can't do what you want to do unless there is a client there to receive it. Marketing is what will bring your tribe and community to you.

Often we think of marketing as a 'sales' tactic, as advertising, and it can have a slightly uncomfortable energy around it for many people. I believe this is because some marketing can feel as if a business is trying to push for a sale and get their potential customers to 'buy into' something. Perhaps you've been on the receiving end of this and it felt uncomfortable to feel as if you were being 'sold to'. There is definitely a stigma around sales sometimes, especially for those in more conscious industries who don't wish to buy into the normal marketing ploys and or come across as pushy in any way. If any of that rings true to you, then I encourage you to start to change the narrative you may hold around it.

Marketing is in fact just another form of communication. It is communicating what you do, who you are, why you do what you do and what you offer, and, most importantly, it is aimed at those who *want* to hear your message and work with you. If you do this well and with authenticity, passion, integrity and commitment, you will be attracting the exact people who *want* and *need* what you are offering – no savvy sales ploy or 'pushing' needed. When you communicate and market yourself well, your ideal clients will come to you and want what you're offering, so the exchange is mutually beneficial and a beautiful, positive experience for all.

Before you begin, it's important to establish who you are trying to communicate with and what it is that you're wanting to share. What is the key message you want to get across and what are you trying to sell or promote? Knowing who your clients are, which you've already been working on in creating your yogi avatar in previous chapters, is the first step to doing this. Then you can begin to look at how they would want to be communicated with, and really feel into that particular demographic for potentially more effective targeted marketing.

This can vary depending on the tribe you're reaching out to, so take your time to consider them. Of course, if you want to keep your marketing more open to a mass audience that can also be totally fine and still work. At the end of the day, if you're clear on your purpose, what you do and are staying true to that, the right people will come.

JOURNALLING MOMENT

- What media streams does your ideal client most likely spend time on? You may know this from observing or from their age range, or you can ask in a survey or do some research if you're unsure.

- Where would they be looking for someone like you or for your offerings? Social media, search engines, word of mouth, local cafes and shops?

- How much time do they have to look for this?

- Where do they spend their time? Cafes, shops, work, online?

- What are their influences?

- What would make them want to practise yoga with you?

- What would they want to see, know about you or feel in order to make that decision?

This can be a very insightful process and can really help you to understand what your marketing needs are and therefore where to spend your time, energy and maybe investment.

Making time for marketing should be a part of your business and work time commitment. The same way you would put time aside to prepare a class, you need to carve out time in your week dedicated to this. Not only will this get your business off the ground, but it will also help to sustain it over time, aid in growing your community, establishing a healthy reputation and maintaining long-term clients.

There is a huge difference between chasing quick sales and building long-term relationships with your clients. The latter is where the focus should be as this is what will grow your business, and will be more rewarding, as you will be connecting with students and seeing them move through their journey as you do yours. It is really an honour to be on this path with your tribe.

So, when you're working on this, you're not only looking at spending time establishing who you are and what you offer, but also retaining clients by nurturing this relationship. You may even find that someone is drawn to work with you but perhaps it isn't aligned right now for whatever reason, although in the future they may become a client in some way and potentially for something even bigger like a retreat or training – you really never know. Therefore, having a longer-term vision is beneficial.

With all of this considered, think about what kind of commitment you're willing to make to market and promote your business. Think of the time and money you put into this as an investment and trust that you will absolutely get back what you put in and more. We are going to look at many ways to help promote your business for free, for a minimal investment, and if you have a marketing budget set aside. All options can work, although they may differ in the speed at which they grow your business, and the reach and speed of impact may vary.

Building a database

One of the main aims of marketing is to sell a product or service but also to build up your database of customers, current and future. Therefore, in any marketing it is vital to be authentic, to maintain your integrity and to be aligned to your mission, and on brand. Every connection point with your clients is an opportunity to gather information, as well as their details, to add to your database.

The reason this is so important is, as mentioned, even if right now they might not want to work with you, if you and what you do resonates with them, they may want to in the future. Therefore, it's important to gather this pool of potential clients so that when new offerings come out, for example, they are all there ready to be tapped into.

Now it's critical to be super clear here that these are people who *want* to be communicated with, they have asked or given consent to be added to your database, shown an interest in your work, and would be grateful to hear from you when you share what you have coming up. This therefore becomes the easiest and possibly most effective way to 'sell' your products or service, because these people have already aligned with you.

TOP TIPS

There are many ways to gather information on potential clients:

- A 'sign up to my newsletter' option on your website. This can be as simple as a click through, or pop up. The wording used can vary, but a call to action here is needed, for example: 'Sign up', 'Join now', 'Yes please'.

- Freebies. This is a well-known strategy and can really work if it resonates with you. For example, share something of value that you wish to 'gift' people who have landed on your website, and to receive this they must enter their details. This can work well as not only do they already wish to receive something of yours, and are therefore interested in what you do, but it also gives you an opportunity to showcase some of your work as a little taster.

- Have a mailing list available at any events, classes and workshops that you do so people can sign up at the end of class.

- Mention your business on social media and invite people to send you their email addresses if they wish to receive newsletters etc.

Transparency is key here. No one wants to feel that they're being sold to, or will be bombarded by daily emails, so letting people know what it is you'll be using this information for is super helpful. For example, explain that you'll only be sending out monthly newsletters with your upcoming events, your latest blog post and so on.

Email marketing

Once you have your database built and growing you can use email marketing, sending out newsletters to help market and promote your business and offerings. This is a great way not only to share what you have coming up, but also to connect with your community and keep the relationship going. Be sure to send out consistent, relevant emails that are coherent with your brand and message.

The newsletters could include:

- Any promotions you have.

- Upcoming events.

- A little personal note to share your journey or some inspiration if that feels relevant to your business and brand.

- Recommendations such as books and podcast you've found inspiring.

- Your latest blog post.

Individual email marketing

You may also choose to communicate via email to help boost your relationship with current clients, connecting with them after they've attended a class or workshop, for example to check in or to offer a free session on their birthday, or perhaps to remind them of something that they've shown an interest in. These might be group emails to those it is relevant to, or even better might be a personal email to an individual whom you know might benefit from it or has shown an interest in something. These personal touches can take time, but are a beautiful way of consciously connecting with your clients and developing a long-term connection with your community. It is these personal touches that make you stand out from the crowd of mass selling, and they are especially relevant if someone is interested in something you're offering that has a long-term commitment, such as a training, or has a high investment cost. The more time and energy you put into these connections, the more your clients will feel seen, heard and valued as customers.

Free marketing

Marketing your business for free can actually be pretty fun and creative. Here are just a few ideas of ways you can do this with great results.

TOP TIPS

- **Offer free classes:** It's immediate, easy and probably one of the most effective ways of promoting yourself – by letting people get a feel for what you do straightaway. Some may shy away from doing anything for free, and although I absolutely understand the reasoning behind this often, such as devaluing yourself, as a one-off to help get you out there and give people a taster for what you do it is perfect. It is a simple exchange of your time and energy for potential client reach.

  Take time spreading the word, using contacts, friends, social media channels, word of mouth and so on to get people in. Think of this as a community event, a way to meet people, chat to them, get to know them, ask them questions. You can use this time to not only communicate what you do, but also learn about what your ideal client wants and needs. This is very valuable time so ask lots of questions. Most importantly, get their contact details to start to build your database.

- **Register on yoga websites:** There are plenty of free directories online and places where you can share what you do, on websites, databases, social media groups and so on. This can be a little time consuming, and it's important to stay active and update regularly, and to check if you've received any messages on that platform; however, it can be very effective.

- **Social media:** This is a free marketing tool in itself and more details can be found on this in the Chapter 5: Social Media.

- **Word of mouth:** This is also a marketing tool, and an incredibly effective one. It's as simple as telling people what you do, and why you do what you do. Share your passion and purpose with the world, with anyone who seems interested and wants to hear.

  One of the best ways to grow the business is to chat to people about it, show your passion and that in itself inspires people to work with you, or try out what it is you have on offer. Show an interest in *them*. Asking people questions and getting to know them on a personal level, and then maybe, if it feels relevant, mentioning what you do from an authentic aligned place, a place of truly wanting to help rather than 'sell', is a beautiful way of growing your community.

- **Collaborations:** This might be working with someone else, being featured on someone's blog, social media, Instagram Live or podcast. This is a great way of getting exposure to an audience who might already be interested in what it is that you do. You might then return the favour, featuring that person, or perhaps sharing what they do on your social media, in your newsletter and so on, so it is beneficial for both parties, as well as usually being pretty fun and inspiring.

Marketing and promotional ideas

If you do have a budget set aside for marketing, even just a small one, there are a number of ways you could use this. Work out what feels most true to you and not only the message you want to share, but where it may serve you best in regard to who it is you want to reach. Where would this investment be best spent to reach your target audience?

- **Paid advertisements:** This can be anything from paid advertisements on social media, such as paying to promote a post or event to promotion on a particular website or in a magazine. Make sure you get an idea of how many people will view this advert, and feel that it's targeting the right people for you.

- **Google Ads:** These are the paid ads on google that help get you seen by the targeted audience in their search. Setting this up can take some time, and the cost can vary as you set your amount yourself, but it has been known to be incredibly effective for many businesses when done well. This means do your research. Be mindful of your words, your call to action, your key words and the target audience you set, as well as your budget per click. All of this will change how effective this is, and how much it will cost you. You can learn more about this on Google Ads itself, which shows you how to use it, and there are multiple opinions and very in-depth articles written on this topic so if this is something you choose to do, do look into ways to get the absolute most from it.

- **Flyers:** These are especially good for someone wanting to promote a local business. As a method, it's a little old school, but flyers actually still work very well, especially when it comes to small local businesses. Local communities want to support their local businesses. It is easy and quick to get some nice simple flyers designed by you, using a simple, free online design platform such as Canva.com, or by someone else, and printed. Make sure they include all the important information and represent your brand. Then share them in the local area, anywhere where you feel your ideal client might spend time. You may even ask other local businesses if they would be okay with you leaving some in there, such as hairdressers, cafes, physiotherapists' offices and so on.

- **Testimonials:** Gathering feedback and testimonials is hugely helpful and these can be used in any of your marketing ventures. You may choose to share a testimonial on your website, in a newsletter or even on social media. Instead of you always promoting what you do, why not let the work speak for itself and let people hear from those who have already experienced it?

Promotions

Offering promotions can really get the ball rolling with a particular course, class, workshop or other projects on offer. It is a nice way of gently enticing people to sign up or join something, and doesn't have to be thought of as a sales tactic. As mentioned before, think of this as calling in the people who *want* and *need* what you're offering. A well-voiced promotion can be the catalyst to them joining if they need a little encouragement.

Here are some promotional ideas:

- **Two for one:** This could be the traditional two classes for the price of one, or you could use this as a model and play with it to find something that feels right for you, such as offering a discount on a bundle or pack of classes.

- **Invite a friend for half price:** This, or something similar, invites the client to share the promotion with someone else. It is a brilliant way of not only letting them feel they're getting more for their money (which of course they are), but also allowing you to share what you do with more people, and they can share their experience with someone too. A beautiful gift of abundance all around!

- **Early bird rates:** These work really well and really give any event, class, course and so on a good boost to get the energy flowing and the bookings coming in.

- **Giveaways and extras:** Sometimes giving a discount or offer doesn't feel right. If this is the case, and yet you still wish to do a promotion of sorts, then adding something extra can be a great solution. For example, 'sign up to this beginners' yoga course and you'll get a brand-new yoga mat to start your yoga journey'. Of course, to be appealing the 'extra' wants to feel relevant and be a genuine incentive.

Chapter 5

SOCIAL MEDIA

'How can you be a bright light among the noise?'

When discussing any business these days it's hard to avoid the topic of social media. It has increasingly become a huge part of daily life for many of us on a personal level, and a valuable tool on a business level. It can bring up mixed opinions regarding our interaction and usage of it in a work scenario; however, there are many upsides to it when used in a conscious and mindful way that feels aligned to you and your business.

If you choose to use social media for your business, and for it to be as effective as possible, it can actually require a lot of effort. People assume that it is easy, yet most likely there will be many hours spent considering a content plan and strategy, creating content and deciding the best ways of interacting with your audience.

In order to be successful on social media, and for it to benefit your business, you need to have a clear understanding of your message and identify the best ways of expressing this. The message you choose to share might be linked to your mission statement, your brand goals and values and your aim as a practitioner and teacher, as well as the specifics of what you do. Being clear about what the message is behind each individual post, as well as the overarching message of your brand, can help you create exciting and meaningful interaction.

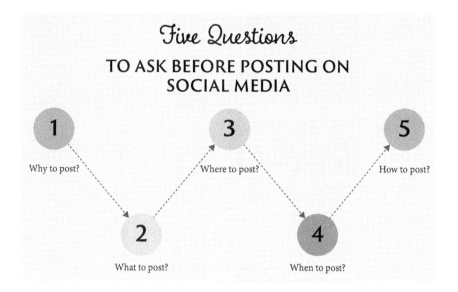

Communication and your voice

Just as we have already looked at previously, I invite you to consider the tone in which you want to engage with your audience on social media, the 'voice' you will be using.

There are a few options:

- Presenting yourself as a brand, which will offer a specific look and feel.

- Presenting yourself as the individual behind the brand, with the look and feel being more personal.

It really is very personal as to which works best for you. You may choose to present yourself very much as a business and brand. This will be dictated by the business you are developing and what is at the core of this. If you are building a bigger business, with multiple employees for example, and very much a brand in how you present yourself, then sticking to that will most likely be the best option. For example, when posting you would say 'we' rather than 'I' and keep to strict brand guidelines in regard to images and words used. This can be done in a very effective way, and even though it may not be as personal, can absolutely attract clients, connect with your community and build a relationship between your audience and the business. The social media account is an extension of the business and is approached very much in that way.

If you see social media as a more personal way of communicating and expressing yourself, then it could be used as a tool to establish a slightly different dynamic with your clients, allowing them to see the 'you', the individual behind the business. Remember that even when we take a more personal approach it is important to still hold certain boundaries in place, from an ethical perspective and also from a business perspective, as of course you will still want to maintain an element of professionalism. However, as long as you are approaching this more personal sharing space from a very authentic space and with integrity behind what you share, then it can be a powerful way to connect with your community.

Authenticity is key when it comes to sharing on social media. The energy and intention behind what you share is felt by those engaging with your content, so keep it real at all times.

JOURNALLING MOMENT

Here are some simple questions that can help you check the intention behind your posts:

- Am I being real and authentic in what I am sharing right now?

- Am I grounded and connected as I share this?

- What part of me wants to share this?

- What is driving me to share this content? To inspire? To educate? To reach out? To promote?

- What am I wanting from my audience in response to this, if anything?

These questions and contemplations are a good filter to help navigate the content you decide to share, and to continue to check in with your *why* and the reasoning behind what you post.

I like to think of what we post on social media as a contribution to a collective space. Rather than it simply being a place to seek validation or solely for promotional purposes, how can we use social media as a channel to contribute something of value to the online realm? There is *so* much out there, social media is saturated in almost every discipline, so how can what you share be a valued contribution to your community, as well as standing out from the crowd? Your voice and what you want to share do matter and are needed, it's just about making sure the content comes from the right place and is curated in a way that can reach the right audience, the audience that *wants* to hear what you have to say.

Sharing content online can be very much a creative process, a form of creative expression if we choose it to be. It can be an outlet for your voice, your message, your creativity through images, photography, words, video and so on. As with any form of creativity, it won't always appeal to everyone. And that is okay. We must remember that we don't always appeal to everyone, resonate with everyone or even be liked by everyone, and that is okay.

So, when you are choosing to share something to a wider audience, especially when it is online and open for the world to see in essence, remember that you are sharing something because you feel called to, and it will land with those that it is meant to. It will speak to the right people – your tribe, your audience, your perfect client – and that is all you need. Share your truth, be authentic in what you share and reach those that you want to reach. Don't worry about the rest.

Establishing a healthy relationship with social media

It can be easy to fall into the comparison trap, especially in the world of social media, so it is vital to stay true and in your own integrity, and follow your own path rather than getting caught up in a potential web of comparison and all that can lead to, such as self-doubt, limiting beliefs and so on.

If you find yourself getting wrapped up in that spiral, notice what it was that started it and question whether that is true and serving you.

Consider becoming more selective with who you follow and are choosing to be influenced by and become conscious of curating the experience you want and can thrive off, even in the world of social media. Establish healthy boundaries for yourself. This really should be practised in all aspects of your work, but is even more true when it comes to social media. In the same way you select who you socialize with in real life, become selective as to who you socialize with online as this will impact your life.

A nice little practice can be to note how you feel after being on social media. Start to be aware of your feelings, emotions and inner dialogue and see if you are inspired and motivated by the experience or you've walked away feeling depleted. Try to become very aware of whose accounts impact you in this way and what types of things deplete you rather than uplift you, and begin to curate your own experience of how you digest your information. Unfollow those who aren't adding to your experience, follow those who inspire you, whom you gain something from whether it be wisdom, insight, humour and so on. Get very conscious and selective of your time on these platforms.

Once you are clear on how you wish to interact and what your relationship with social media is then it can be a very creative, exciting and fruitful extension of your business and yourself. However, as with everything in life and work, organization, intention and productivity are key. Therefore what follows are some things to consider, work through and apply in order to get the most from your use of social media and help grow your business.

It's interesting to note that the algorithm and ways in which various social media platforms work change frequently, so rather than being very specific in ways of working the system to gain more followers, I have stuck to the more general approach of building your brand on social media, gaining the followers you want and using it in the most effective way. These are not 'social media hacks' as these are constantly being changed and updated to work the algorithm, and if that is something you are interested in I recommend doing some research into what works for your specific needs at this moment. The following, however, apply to anyone and everyone and who wishes to gradually build a real online presence that is more aligned to the idea of quality over quantity.

What social media?

There are endless social media platforms now, and I won't be going into each every single one but instead focusing on some of the most commonly used ones. You may choose to use only one, or you may choose to be on all, it really is up to you.

Once again, quality over quantity is key, so if you feel that having many platforms to engage with will mean you are not as engaged or productive on any of them, then it could be more beneficial to stick to using fewer or even just one that you are very engaged with and can really make the most of. You could choose to link your various social media platforms so that when you post on one it automatically shares on another. It is possible to do this on some platforms, but not all. This may affect the engagement as different platforms will benefit from posts at different times, but it absolutely can work and save time. Pre-scheduling and setting your posts to go live can also be a good timesaver.

I also recommend exploring the possibility of having a dedicated social media person to help you. As with a designer, having someone who is dedicated, knowledgeable and focused on creating and developing your social media could be a valuable investment for the growth of your business. A business or freelancer who specializes in this can really add much value, utilizing their expertise with a focused desired outcome, such as getting more followers, driving sales and so on.

Alternatively, a lot of people want to be in control of their own social media for their business, so you might not feel comfortable completely delegating this to someone else, especially if you are more spontaneous and frequent with your posts and it is more about live and in-the-moment sharing of your world.

Here are some social media platforms you might consider:

- **Facebook:** The biggest social media platform, this uses all types of media – text, images and video as well as live elements. It is good for sharing events, sharing in groups and building connections with your audience.

- **Instagram:** Used for sharing images, captions, stories and live elements, it is good for sharing information, interacting with your audience and growing your following.

- **Twitter:** Used for shorter 'tweets' (captions), but for an older, more dominantly male audience. It is often used for news updates and public relations.

- **YouTube:** Used for sharing video content, this can build a following. It is good for building brand awareness and sharing educational or interesting content through the media or film. It has a big audience with a wide range.

- **TikTok:** Good for fun or educational interaction through short videos, this mostly appeals to a younger audience.

- **LinkedIn:** Used predominantly for business connections and networking.

There are of course many more, and more coming on the scene all the time.

I'm not going to focus too much on any one particular platform, however, and instead will share about social media use in general, the best way you can use it for your brand, top tips, engagement and so on that could be relevant on all platforms where applicable.

Tips, tools and how-tos

Scheduling

One of the main things to consider when using social media is the scheduling of posts and the frequency of posting. In order to gain a following, have a wider reach, grow your engagement with your audience and ultimately access those who would love to benefit from your services, there are some key things to consider:

- **Consistency:** This is absolutely key in growing your online business and social media accounts. Consistency not only shows a sense of commitment to your followers, but it builds a familiarity, a connection with them and them with you. The more followers see you, the more likely they are to begin to engage and as they do so are more inclined to want to be a part of what you offer.

A consistent presence also helps with the algorithms with social media accounts, which will mean that more people are inclined to see your posts and your profile, and know who you are and what you offer.

- **Timing:** The timing of your post can greatly influence the number of people who see it. You need to analyse your audience and the engagement you get to determine the best times to post. Don't forget that these times will vary from platform to platform.

- **Planning:** Having an overall social media plan or strategy in place can help not only to give you an overarching vision for your social media, but also to map your posting. Developing a map or calendar dedicated to this can be very useful. You might want to list what you want to promote when, depending on what you have coming up or where your focus might be, and to keep on track with your consistency and flow. A monthly plan can really help, especially if you are prepping your posts in advance, or even scheduling them. Of course, this may change as you go and if you want to share a post spontaneously, but having something set out with a desired outcome, focus and structure is incredibly helpful. I recommend taking the time at the start of each month to plan this out, with your calendar close by to see what might need more marketing when. You can then spend a dedicated time editing your photos, writing copy and maybe scheduling your posts for the optimal time. As you do this you can see how each image or post will look all together, so you can plan the overall theme and make sure it flows well, looks good, honours your brand message and story and so on. If social media is your primary marketing focus then taking the time to do this each month is essential, and checking in on it, adjusting it if necessary and seeing the responses regularly throughout the month, is equally crucial to the success of your social platforms.

Theme

Having an overall theme for your social media can be an interesting way of keeping it aligned with your brand and overall message. I like to think of Instagram, for example, as an instant insight into the essence of your business. In the same way you did when you were looking at the branding, try to keep a coherent theme throughout your social media page, whether it be through images, tone and so on, that looks thought through rather than randomly posted. Your audience likes to know that you've put time and care into what you are sharing and there is a purpose behind it.

To keep some consistency try:

- posting a video once a week

- having a 'theme of the week' that is a point of discussion and focus

- once a week doing a 'live' with your audience.

There are many ways to curate this, but having an overall theme can heighten your page, help people know what to expect from it and therefore what they'll get if they follow you. This structure will also help you when it comes to planning your social media schedule, rather than having to think about it each day as it comes.

Creating engaging content

- **Quality:** Quality counts. The average consumer is getting more and more social media savvy, meaning that any average post probably won't go that far in really generating much interest or interaction. And when I say interest, I really mean from your potential clients or students, not just your close network of friends. Quality is more important than ever, and really doesn't have to be difficult to achieve. Technology has made it very possible to get great content to share nowadays. This means actually taking your time to create your content, to take a considered photo which is clear, looks good and is edited to your brand vibe if need be. Whatever it is, it has to say something and show the care you have put in.

- **Relevance:** Sharing relevant content on your social media is a must. If someone has chosen to follow you based on the topics you focus on in your posts, then bear in mind that *that* is *why* they are following you. If you were to suddenly post something a bit random that is not relevant to you or your brand, you may be at risk of losing some followers and potential students.

Writing copy

The benefits of dedicating time to create quality content also applies to the copy or captions used. Creating captivating copy is a skill in itself and can take time to develop but here are some things to consider to help you on your way:

- **Be authentic:** This comes back to your purpose, your essence, your mission statement and your brand. Can you stay true to these in your copy? Always consider your tone of voice and the way in which you want to engage and 'speak' to your clients. **Keep it simple and clear:** What is your message in *this* post? What is the purpose? What do you really want to say and how can you say it? **Be personal:** People want to know *you*. They want to know the person behind the 'account' or brand. If you feel comfortable with it then don't be afraid to get personal. This can be anywhere from sharing your own story of how you got to where you are, what you learned along the way, to your journey right now and what you're currently navigating. **Be engaging:** This is the core element to writing interesting and appealing copy, yet not always the easy bit. Here are some tips on ways to make your copy juicy and engaging.

  - **Ask questions:** Get your audience engaged by asking them questions that will prompt them to comment and be part of the conversation on your social media.

  - **Be bold:** Writing a bold or opening line can really capture your audience. This could be something that shocks them, gets them intrigued and curious or really stops someone in their tracks.

For example, *'It's time I share my secret with you...'* And then go on to post about something personal that feels relevant and will resonate with your followers. This will instantly make someone want to engage and read what you have shared, and if it has touched something in them, then they'll probably interact with it in some way through a like, a comment, or sometimes even a private message.

- **Be a source of information:** Offer something of real value, such as some useful information that they will want to read, because they need and want this wisdom. For example, share insightful anatomy of a yoga pose, maybe with a specific audience in mind such as runners. Or perhaps your posts and offerings are aimed at women's connection with their menstrual cycle, and therefore you frequently share information and tips on this. Consistently offering insightful wisdom on a specific topic will generate a solid following from a particular group that it is aimed at, building their trust in you as a reliable source of information.

Images

If you're choosing to use platforms that are more visual, such as Instagram or TikTok, then the images you use are the focal point and will be as important as your caption. As with your copy, you want your images to be relevant and of high quality. This does not necessarily mean using loads of heavy filters and editing everything a lot. In fact, sometimes over-editing can have an inauthentic feel. However, taking care and creating beautiful images that are thought through and curated mindfully and with a particular vibe will produce a more appealing and inviting profile.

A few tips on images:

- **Quality:** This means making sure your images are clear, high resolution and often simple is best.

- **Consistency:** As with the copy, there wants to be an element of consistency with your images that is also connected to the look and feel of your brand. This might be in regard to the content of your images, the 'vibe' and feel of them, or the way in which you edit them. One simple way of doing this could be to use the same tone or filter on them all, or to frame your images in a similar way each time.

- **Editing:** The general rule of thumb is not to over-edit. However, spending some time enhancing them a little can help your images stand out and look more professional. This can be small tweaks such as brightening the image a little, playing with the contrast or saturation, sharpening the image or doing a few touch-ups. Often, the more natural, the better.

- **Natural lighting:** In general, photos, especially of people, are more flattering taken in natural light. If you want to get the most from your images, then taking photos during the golden hour, as it's known, at sunrise and sunset, usually produces the best lighting.

- **Framing:** The thoughtful framing of a photo can help it look more professional. You may want the main subject to be in the centre as the focal point, but sometimes using the *rule of thirds* can create a more interesting image. This is achieved by using the grid lines available on the camera on most social media platforms and aligning the subject of the photo to one of the lines so it's off-centre.

A few tips on videos:

- **Quality:** As with images, your videos want to have high-quality content, meaning good images, high resolution and clear audible sound.

- **Editing:** With just a few small edits you can make your videos look much more professional. As with your images, simple editing is usually best, such as adding an opening title screen, placing your logo somewhere or including a screen at the end with your website and contact details.

- **Character:** The beautiful thing about using video content is that it provides an opportunity to show your character to a greater extent. You can use this in many different ways, perhaps sharing more serious videos, offering some insights or being more personal by talking to camera, posting a yoga flow, or even a fun TikTok that is playful and entertaining. Feel in to you and what your brand would align to and let yourself be creative with this process and enjoy this way of connecting with people that can be more alive than a still image or caption.

- **Caption:** Adding captions to videos can be helpful, depending on what it is and what it is being used for. If you're posting information, educational videos or teaching videos, for example, then captions can help them to be more user-friendly, making them more likely to be watched multiple times and even shared.

Interaction

The level of interaction and posting will be personal and depend on the time you wish to spend on social media. If you are seeing social media as your main advertising tool, and the way in which you reach most of your desired clients, then you need to spend time on this. In the same way you would dedicate time to marketing your business, you should spend time on your social media in order to see the growth. The way you interact with your audience, and the speed at which you do so, can have a positive impact. Replying to comments quickly, taking the time to reply to private messages and even sharing on your 'Story' for example, for those platforms where that is applicable, are all great ways to generate more engagement with your followers.

Insights

Getting insights and analysing your results on your social media is incredibly helpful. There are specific websites and platforms that can assist with this, and on some social media platforms themselves you can look into how your posts are doing, what your engagement is like and so on. This can be very useful in showing you what content has the best engagement, on what days and times posts generate the best interaction, and what the general demographic is. Based on this, you can start to tailor your social media plan accordingly for the best results for your brand and the best engagement with your desired audience.

Chapter 6

YOUR CLASSES

'Dare to leave your mark with everything you do.'

As we've already seen, within the yoga industry there are many ways in which you can navigate your career. The business opportunities and paths you can take are endless and it would be impossible to cover all potentials in this book; however, we will look at a few of the most common options and ways in which you can get going. Think of this as a starting place for your potential business plan, with some insight into a few areas, rather than a deep dive-in. There will be things to consider before you start, as well as tips to get you on your way towards building your dream business.

First, we're going to look at starting your own classes or courses. If you're choosing to set up your own classes, courses or workshops, then there are a few initial points I invite you to contemplate. Some of these we have already covered, but I will repeat for clarity and emphasis as they are vital for these next steps, and much like our asana, the more we repeat the better and clearer we become.

JOURNALLING MOMENT

- Consider first...

    - What are you wanting to create? Is it a weekly offering? A one-off? A course?

- Will it be in person or online?

- Is it specialized or more open?

- Will it be drop-ins or pre-booked?

• Think about who this offering is for. This will most probably be your ideal client, but could vary, so be clear about who you are targeting.

• What is this offering aiming to do? What is your intention and what do you want people to walk away from it with? For example, if you're looking to start a weekly Friday evening yoga class in your local area, what do you want students to get from this class? Be really specific. Think about what the needs of your potential students are and how you can best support them with your offerings.

So using the example of a Friday evening class in your local area, it could be that your ideal client will be coming home from work, winding down from a stressful week, looking to stretch, relax and melt into the weekend. Maybe they'll want to sweat it out and flow, or they'd benefit from a more nurturing practice and long savasana, and so on. Have a think about what *they* would need in that moment of their week. This is so important as it will help you really think about the offering, the timing, the length, what you can call it and who it's aimed at, which will then help you with the marketing and promoting of it and attract the perfect students.

How much time are you willing to commit?

This can be in regard to the time per week that you have to put into this class/course. Don't forget to include planning time, promoting, logistics, organizing and liaising with students, and travel, as well as setting up and packing up time. So even if it's just a one-hour class you want to set up, be realistic about the actual time this class will need in regard to your time commitment each week and feel in to what is possible for you. Be mindful to do this each time you create a new offering so that you're prepared and have the energy to support it, and also that you don't over-commit and then either have to stop, or don't have enough energy to truly honour it. Unfortunately, this is a pitfall we can often fall into when we get started or want to start something new as we are full of enthusiasm for it. There is, however, something to be said for starting slowly and letting something grow organically, once you have a realistic felt experience for what it takes to get a new project going and sustain it.

The offering

Feeling clearer on what your offering might be? Great! Now to really bring this into fruition you might want to consider the following areas.

Research

If you already have a specific area or student in mind, do some research as to what is already on offer for them and what they would benefit most from. Research is essential for any business, to gain a better perspective on what is needed, as well as an understanding of what is already out there. I don't generally like to use the term 'competition', as I believe there is a place for everyone and all offerings, but understanding what is already out there from a business perspective is intelligent. Getting information as to what works time wise, for pricing and so on will enable you to avoid clashing with another class and you can ascertain where there are gaps that you could fill so as not to be in direct competition with another teacher. Alternatively, if you discover that there is a class that is always full you will know that there is more demand from this particular group of clients, and so you could offer an additional option for them.

Location

Always check out the area you're planning to work in. What is already going on in that area? What type of people live there and what are their movements like? If you want to have local exposure, then where will you find most of your students?

For example, if your ideal clients are mums, then think about their routine – what time do they drop their children off at school and where are the local schools? People generally always go with convenience, so perhaps you would aim to position yourself well for these clients by offering a class at the right time for them to come straight after the school run, and to not be too far off the school run route so that it's easy for them and their busy lives. If, however, you're wanting to teach a power flow class to young professionals, then it might be a case of thinking about what time of day works best for them, before or after work, and what location could draw them in.

As with anything mentioned in this section, if you're not sure, ask around. Gather information and do some research to help you make decisions from a well-thought-through and felt space.

Once you've gathered some insight, then it's time to start looking into venues and locations that could work for your teaching. As always, consider your ideal client and the type of location that would appeal to them.

Take a moment and picture your class or course. Feel into it. What does it look like? Who is there? What is the venue like that allows for the perfect setting for what you're offering, and appeals to these students?

TOP THINGS TO CONSIDER

- **Location:** Is it easy to get to, convenient for your student and your allocated time?

- **Transport:** Is it near public transport and does it have parking nearby?

- **Costs.**

- **Availability:** And consistency of this availability if you want an ongoing offering.

- **What else is being offered at this location?** Is it complementary to what you want to offer?

- **Look and feel of the space:** Does this fit with your brand and business?

- **General vibe:** For example, is it luxury, new, fresh, rustic? Does this suit your brand, business and dream clients?

- **External sounds:** Are there any external sounds that might interrupt what you're doing? Be sure to ask about this, especially if you're viewing the venue at a different time from when your class will actually be running. Many times I've heard of someone seeing a venue that was beautiful and peaceful, and so they've booked it, only to find out in the first class that at the same time there's a choir, for example, practising next door that, beautiful as it is, could interrupt the class and compromise the students' overall experience. So, be sure to ask what else is happening in the building at the time you want to run your class.

- **Sound quality:** Check the acoustics of the room and if they work for you, especially if it's a big space and you plan on playing any music.

- **Temperature:** This is an easy one to forget but *so* important as it can really make or break an experience. A class could be absolutely wonderful, but if it's freezing in the space, the chances are the students won't relax and may not have a pleasurable experience.

- **Storage:** If you are planning on running a regular class then it could be helpful to check for storage space to maybe store your props and equipment.

- **Lighting and ambience:** Again, this will depend on your brand and the type of experience you want your students to have, but in general aim to make your clients feel as comfortable and welcome as possible. Lighting can have a huge impact on a space and really change the feel of it. If the lighting is too bright or too dark, for example, you could always consider buying some nice lamps to create your own ambience or playing around with what you have there to change it slightly. Smell could also be considered here and it might be worth checking if it's okay to burn candles, incense and so on in the space you're using, again to create a certain environment for your offering. If not, then there are some really lovely natural cleansing sprays you can use in a space not only to shift any energy that needs clearing to prepare your space, but also to add a nice smell to help students relax and rest. All of these little touches can make a huge difference to the clients' experience and won't go unnoticed.

If you find a lovely venue but are a little unsure, it's always worth asking some potential students what their thoughts are on it. Does the location work for them to get to easily? You may even want to see if the venue is open to a trial while you get started and get the class going. Many places are very amenable to this as they too want the right fit with what is being offered in their space. It is also always worth asking for support and, if it is a community space, finding out ways they may be able to help you promote your classes either through the venue itself or perhaps through some of the other classes being offered in the same place. You may even want to see what else is being offered there and reach out to the other practitioners, introduce yourself and tell them about your offerings to see if there could be any cross-promoting or supporting of each other in any way.

Once all the logistics of location and timings are confirmed then the focus can be on the actual offering itself, the details, description and so on.

JOURNALLING MOMENT

- What is the offering?

- What do you want to name it?

- How do you plan on promoting it?

- What will appeal to others?

- Most importantly, is it aligning with your purpose and mission statement?

- Does it excite you?

- Do you feel passionate about sharing this?

Always check in with this. If it's lighting you up inside to share this offering, that is a great sign that you are on the right track, that it is needed, that it is aligned and that you'll put the energy and commitment into it that is required to get it going. Your passion will drive it forwards and your clients will also feel that love and authenticity and be even more drawn to it – it's the law of attraction, and passion really does attract people.

Online classes

With the Covid-19 pandemic we saw the world change dramatically, and the way in which yoga was being offered had to shift, for many, from an in-person to a virtual experience online. Most teachers chose to or had to move their offerings online, and many are now keeping the silver lining of this part of their newly evolved business. I would therefore like to touch on what it could look like to have a solely, predominantly, or at least partially, online yoga business.

Live online classes

For many teachers, this will mainly be offering live online classes. This can be fairly simple to set up with the use of one of the many online platforms from which you can live stream your classes. Many of us now are familiar with using video call platforms and so forth, and these can easily be used for classes.

TOP TIPS

Some things to bear in mind before starting your online classes:

- Create a nice, quiet and ambient space to teach from.

- Consider the positioning of your camera so that your students can see you clearly and easily and are able to follow your demonstrations and flows with ease.

- Check your sound quality and make sure they can hear you clearly, with no background disruption. You may need to invest in good wireless headphones which are enough for a one-and-a-half-hour class; for a longer offering you might need a head mic.

- Be clear in your information pack as to when the class will begin, how you will send the link to join, what they will need to be prepared for the practice, and anything else you wish to let them know.

- If you have any playlist to accompany the practice, check that your voice can be clearly heard over it, or send them the playlist in advance for them to play during the practice in the background.

- If you choose to use an instrument, harmonium, singing bowls or guitar, then it is essential to consider a high-quality mic and mixer as a bare minimum. Do your research on this as the equipment needed varies depending on the instrument you will use.

- Check your equipment. This may be an investment you choose to make to ensure that you have absolutely the best quality live classes possible. You may choose to have a camera, lighting, microphones and so on.

- Each time you teach, beforehand make sure your software has done its updates and you have switched on 'do not disturb mode' if you are using your phone as a camera.

> • Before you teach, make sure you do a sound check to note that
>   your audio is working well.

Pre-recorded online content and more

You may choose not to offer live classes, but instead to have pre-recorded online content, an online course that is downloaded, classes that can be viewed online on your website or elsewhere, or a combination of the these. This can be presented in many ways, as one-off offerings, a package or programme, or maybe even a membership that your students can buy into to have access to these online offerings and classes. As with anything, it's important to consider what feels alive and aligned for you. With live classes, you have the opportunity to connect and interact with students, whereas with anything pre-recorded you do not; however, the time commitment and potential for reselling is different of course. These are all things to bear in mind when looking at your options.

With pre-recording content, a lot of the same tips mentioned for live online classes apply. In addition, you may want to consider other options for filming, for example if you want to use multiple cameras or angles. You can also of course edit your recordings when they are not live, either to make the viewing more interesting or to show more options. In the edit. you could also choose to add information, captions, logos or anything else that might be useful.

One-to-one classes

Offering bespoke one-to-one yoga classes can be a very fulfilling way to teach, and also a great business model. Teaching private yoga classes, for many teachers, is where they can potentially make the most income and is the most lucrative part of their business in regard to their time.

I have taught one-to-one yoga classes since I completed my initial teacher training, and it has been a consistent part of my offering since for many reasons. Although a few teachers they may not fully enjoy teaching in this way – after all not everything is for everyone – for most it is very rewarding. I believe this is because you can build a personal rapport with your client, tailoring the classes to their individual needs and supporting them fully. The focused dedication and time you can offer them in sessions can be life-changing for many clients. Receiving this kind of support, having a practice made for them, their abilities, emotional needs, injuries and so on, as well as simply having space held for them in this way by a facilitator, can have a huge impact.

When teaching one-to-one I highly recommend taking the time to have a thorough initial chat before starting, where you can gain information on their health, any injuries or illnesses, stress levels, lifestyle, how they sleep, maybe a bit about any challenges they face in life at the moment as well as what they hope to get from their session with you. You may even want to ask them what their ideal outcome would be from, let's say, a six-month programme working with you. This gives you not only plenty of insight into them and what they will benefit from most in their sessions and how you can support them, but also an idea of what you can work towards together and a rough structure of sessions and how they can develop over time. It is also excellent to be able to track a student's progress in this way, every now and then checking in on how they are doing, especially if you've been working on something specific like back pain, or trouble sleeping. This is helpful for you as a teacher to see how they are progressing and what is working and what isn't, but also can be encouraging for them to see their progress over time and this will help them stay committed to their yoga journey.

From a business perspective, you can usually charge quite a bit more for one-to-one sessions. Make sure you take into consideration not only the length of the class itself, but travel time and costs (if you are going to them), planning sessions and maybe even follow-up time and any communication you may have supporting them in between sessions. This will vary person to person and depend on what you feel comfortable with.

Some teachers happily offer frequent support to their students, checking in between sessions, maybe offering a yoga practice, video or class plan they can do to help with their consistency and journey. You could even create a model in which all of your one-to-ones have access to some videos or a membership of some sort that allows them to develop their practice further. Of course, all of this should be taken into consideration as part of your offering and therefore your costs.

In regard to pricing, as with regular classes, do some research as to what the going rate is in the area and take into consideration how you value your time. You may want to offer complimentary classes for those interested, and then have a set price per session, and maybe a price if they want to commit to a package, most likely with a discount if that is what they choose. A sliding scale is a great way of doing this, so the more classes in the package they buy, the cheaper it becomes per session.

This, of course, encourages students to commit to more classes, but you may wish to put in terms and conditions in regard to the completion of this package – for example, all classes must be used within six months, so that there is a boundary around usage.

As private sessions can be a little more ad hoc, unlike weekly classes in a studio, it is worth having a cancelation policy in place so that you can make sure you are always able to fill up your time. This is especially important if your income is dependent on this. With that in mind, it is also worth asking clients to commit to weekly sessions and have a set time and day they are booked in for, so that you can calculate your weekly revenue more easily, and if they cancel at least have enough notice to offer this split to someone else.

Promoting one-to-ones may require a specific marketing strategy in itself and I recommend making it clear in your classes, on your website and social media that this is part of your offering. Simple mentions during a group class, or in the caption of a social media post can help get the word out there that you offer this. Once you have secured a few clients, encourage them to share with their friends and let them know if you're looking for more students as the chances are, if they are your target client (yogi avatar), they will know other people who are also your target client and would love sessions with you. Word of mouth is one of the best marketing strategies, so show up, offer amazing sessions and let them share the praise and help promote you organically.

—— *Chapter 7* ——

OTHER OFFERINGS

'Sharing your purpose in life is the greatest act of service.'

Now that we've covered a bit about starting your own classes or teaching at studios, it's time to look at other potential offerings in the yoga industry, delving into the world of retreats, workshops and corporate yoga and what it takes to get these going. Both retreats and workshops could be considered more intensive offerings in comparison to classes. For many students and clients these will be a step deeper in their own personal journey in yoga, as well as being pretty powerful for your own evolution as a teacher too, in regard to what they invite you to get into.

Space holding for a workshop or even more for a retreat is a beautiful and mammoth task and is not something to jump into too quickly no matter how exciting it might sound. Of course, it is a wonderful invitation to expand and grow in your work, and is exciting indeed, when the time is right. As with any developments in your career and what you offer, make sure you are absolutely ready for this and all that it might bring. It can be very easy to get caught up in the adventure and appeal of running a retreat, especially if it is in a beautiful location; however, I say from much experience, it is definitely not a holiday and even though it may be an incredible experience, it is one that demands a lot of energy, presence, experience and capacity to hold space for all the people who are attending.

When looking at workshops, it is a very different story. Although it can still take a lot more of your energy to hold the space, offer the in-depth information, take people on a journey, or whatever it is you have planned for your workshop topic, because it is usually over a shorter length of time, it is one that can often be felt into sooner as a yoga teacher. For some teachers, this may even be straightaway as their main offering and what they do.

Creating a workshop

The beautiful thing about workshops is that they open the space for a deeper dive into your work, maybe providing a laser sharp look at something you are really passionate about sharing, or simply giving you more time to take people further in their experience and learn something in more detail. This also means that you can really enjoy the extended time, open up to your creativity in your work, and share all that you wish to share on this topic or in this journey, without the constriction of only having an hour or so with your clients.

A workshop may just be a few hours, or could run over a few days – it really depends on the topic and what your aim is. As the name suggests, a workshop is an opportunity to 'workshop' an idea, to explore a specific area perhaps or get really absorbed in a theme. This could be navigated in a number of ways, depending on the style of yoga you teach or the type of teacher you are, and of course it will most likely be linked with your mission statement. The most important piece is, as always, to start with the *why*. Why are you offering this workshop and what is its core theme or aim?

I would suggest, in general, that you offer workshops once you've already built up a regular clientele who are ready for more from you. Often students need a few classes, at least, with a teacher to start to get a 'feel' for them, and then be ready to go deeper into a topic with this particular facilitator. As workshops tend to be longer in regard to the actual session, so too is the time needed to prepare them, and naturally the rate you charge needs to reflect that. For people to 'buy in' to a slightly bigger investment with you, it is fair to say that they have most likely already come across you or know you somehow. More experience as a teacher also allows you to have got to grips with teaching and holding space, and potentially means that you are more prepared to hold a workshop space.

Of course, this isn't always the case and some teachers may dive straight into offering workshops because they're super passionate about something reality specific or are naturally really good at it and at teaching in that way.

We all have our unique talents, and flowing with that is, above all, the most important thing. For example, a teacher who, new or more experienced, is really talented at arm balances and the biomechanics of arm balances, might want to run a workshop on arm balances and be totally capable of sharing this information, whether they've been teaching one month or one decade. If it is coming from an authentic, experienced and embodied place then it should feel right to offer this topic as an 'expert' in this more in-depth setting. The key with any workshop, or any class for that matter, is to have totally embodied it and integrated it enough to be able to teach it, share it and hold space for it from a place of absolute truth, integrity and a real desire to share it. As with anything you offer, it should align with you, where you are at and your core mission as a teacher.

In today's climate, it's also fair to say that some people may only ever offer workshops. Leading workshops could be your sole business offering and, as many people have proven, this can be incredibly successful. There really is no one way for anyone's business and so if that feels true to you then that is perfect. There are plenty of people who have established great businesses by only leading workshops in their home town or even travelling the world doing so, offering maybe one specialist, carefully curated workshop that they get known for worldwide.

If you decide that your work will be workshop focused, it is key that your promoting and marketing are done in such a way to really hone in on this. As you won't be building your clients for workshops from your weekly classes and so on, a slightly different marketing plan is needed in order to boost exposure and get the right students for you through the door. This is, of course, totally possible, and nowadays with social media, I've seen this done very effectively. You may even choose to only run your workshops online for example, in which case again the way in which you build your client base will be totally different, but still absolutely possible. It's simply a case of looking at it differently and making sure your branding and marketing align with this.

So, let's look at how to develop your workshop. As with every other aspect of your business, it needs to connect with your mission statement, your values and your gifts as a teacher. If there is one main thing you would love students to get from this time with you, what would it be?

Of course, the themes for your workshops may change as you may choose to offer many over time, but each time you decide to create one and put it out there, I invite you to sit with these questions. Always start with the *why*. Why does this workshop need to be offered and who would benefit from it?

As I mentioned before, developing workshops can be creative and fun and will most likely push you as a teacher to look deeper into something yourself, clean up your knowledge on a topic or think of interesting ways to develop a theme. While workshops allow for creativity and collaboration, leaving room for flexibility and change as the sessions progress, many teachers like to leave much of it to intuition and see what comes from the collective in the space.

When coming up with your topic or theme, ask yourself what is needed. If you know who the ideal student would be for this workshop, consider what they would benefit from more of, what their needs might be at this time, what they are ready to step into or develop, or perhaps what challenges they have and how your workshop could serve in healing these.

Creating workshops can be approached in a number of ways. They may be more anatomically focused, asana focused or more theme based, spiritually aligned or targeted to a specific group of people, such as new mums.

Here are some examples of more anatomical approaches:

- If your yogi avatar and ideal client are new to yoga, then a beginners' workshop is a fantastic offering. What do they need? Basics, clarity and the foundations for their yoga practice. The workshop could then be a simple look at some of the main asana in yoga classes, or a breaking down of the sun salutation in which you really slow it down and clean up the structure for them so they can feel more confident, safe and empowered in their classes moving forwards.

- For some athletic yogis, perhaps it would be a dive into arm balances. Again, think about what they might need, want and be enticed to know more about. You could do a whole workshop on getting over the fear of being upside down, or the anatomy of handstands, or make it super fun and playful and bring out the childlike quality of arm balances to help demystify them and encourage people to explore them more and give them a go, with the anatomy and experience to help.

- You may choose to build a workshop specifically for people with a particular ailment or injury. For example, a workshop to help with back pain in which you focus on how to adapt your practice to help support back pain, as well as offering a tailor-made practice to alleviate this issue and perhaps some movements, poses and so on that can be a great support to this.

If you choose to create a workshop based more on a theme, much like many classes are created, there are endless possibilities you could explore, so feel into what inspires you.

Here are some examples of more theme-based workshop ideas:

- **Seasonal workshops:** Workshops based on the seasonal changes and how yoga can support the body, mind and soul and nourish students during the seasons.

- **De-stress workshops:** These are always popular, as many people need help to de-stress, release anxiety and tension and find inner peace.

- **Philosophy:** Workshops based on yoga philosophy, sutras, various gods or goddesses and so on.

With the endless options available, enjoy getting creative, feel into what inspires you, what you feel passionate about sharing, and have fun with it.

Once you have your concept in mind for *what* you want to offer in your workshop, then actually creating it and putting it out there is your next step. As with setting up your own classes, there are many things to take into consideration with workshops.

JOURNALLING MOMENT

- Who is this workshop aimed at?

- When would be the best time for them to do this workshop?

- Where would they want to experience this?

- What kind of investment would they be comfortable with, in regard to both time and cost?

- How many people do you want to sign up? Think about the energy in the space and having it full, but also maybe not having so many bodies that it feels too much to hold in the space.

- Take into consideration your time and costs and what feels like a comfortable exchange for you energetically.

- How long will you need to create this and promote it?

Once you have a better understanding of the *what, why, who, when* and *where* for your workshop then you can look at booking a space, contacting a studio or setting it up online. Don't be afraid to think outside the box and maybe even approach corporates, communities and other spaces that may be interested in what you have to offer. Consider your workshop as a product in itself, which can be reproduced and repeated in various places or even in the same place if it's been popular. If something is working then you may not have to tweak it, but instead could grow it, create a series of similar workshops or expand it in other ways.

Write out a small description of your proposed workshop and share it with any places you want to use or approach, or maybe collaborate with. If you can give them an idea of what it is you want to do, they'll be more likely to be enticed and keen to collaborate.

I also recommend having a short bio at hand that can be sent with the proposed workshop description. This will not only cover who you are and what you do, but why you are passionate about sharing this workshop. Explain how this particular topic is close to your heart and your purpose and that is why you would love to share it with people in more depth in a workshop setting. People are drawn to those who are deeply passionate and committed to what it is they are sharing, especially if it is in a workshop setting and they want to learn more about this specific thing.

For promoting and marketing your workshop you'll need a description of it and what it is about. I recommend having one short version that can be used on a flyer or a social media post, for example, and then a longer version in which you go into more detail on your website, or the studio website where you will be teaching it. You'll also most likely want an image or photo to use for promotion – this could be of you but it doesn't have to be.

TIPS FOR WRITING COPY FOR WORKSHOPS

In the longer version of your workshop blurb you might want to go into more depth. Here are some areas to include:

- What this workshop will offer in regard to the theme, topic and journey.

- Why you want to share this work. Write a bit about you and what about this particular topic inspires you and resonates with you and why you feel you are qualified and equipped to share this.

- Who it is aimed at, for example, 'This workshop is for you if you...' or 'Are you in need of some...'

- Who it is not aimed at.

- What your students will walk away with.

- The expectations and desires of your students.

- What students might learn or experience during the workshop.

- Details and logistics – length, dates, investment, location, do they need to bring anything etc.

There is more detail on promoting your workshops in Chapter 4: Marketing and Promotions.

Creating a retreat

Retreats may be my favourite thing to offer and have personally been my main teaching focus throughout my career. I can therefore very confidently tell you that as rewarding as they can be for a facilitator, they are not something to rush into for many reasons.

First, they are, aside from teaching a training, probably the most intensive and demanding offering for a teacher. This is not just in regard to time, but also energetically and in holding the space and a safe container for the work over a longer duration. It can often take teachers many years to develop the skills and build the confidence and experience needed to be able to do this safely, comfortably and with ease.

A retreat also usually requires a lot more content than a yoga practice. For a full and wholesome journey for students on a retreat, often you have to facilitate more than just a daily yoga class and include, for example, meditation, breathwork, different styles of yoga, yoga nidra, kirtan yoga and so on. This isn't essential, of course, and many lovely retreats are just focused on yoga asana; however, having these other options can enable students to get a more from a full retreat and experience some practices they may not have previously encountered.

Organizing a retreat can be quite a big task in itself, with many more logistics involved than anything else you may offer, and so do bear that in mind. Financially they can be risky, as the majority of venues require a deposit, so you really want to make sure you feel confident you'll fill it before you push 'go' on the venture.

All that being said, they really are wonderful and a very potent journey to take people on. If you feel called to lead retreats and it is what makes your heart sing, then the juice is worth the squeeze as it were, and when facilitated well they can be life-changing experiences for students.

If teaching retreats feels absolutely right for you, take some time to feel in to the many routes you could take to make this happen in your career. If the inner adventurer is calling out, then heading off to teach a season at a retreat venue is a brilliant option. This is similar, in a way, to teaching at a studio in that you are hired as the teacher to facilitate and the rest is done by the venue itself. The venue takes care of the bookings and financial responsibilities and you are free to focus on the teaching without those pressures – if you're just starting out, this can be an excellent way in!

There are thousands of venues around the world looking for teachers to do just this, so have a search and see what is out there. I've come across a variety of ways in which this works, and each venue will have a different expectation and offering, but many provide accommodation and food and a small fee for teaching a number of classes a week to their guests. If you're looking to dive headfirst into teaching, are ready for a little adventure and excited by the retreat lifestyle then this can be an amazing experience not just as a teacher but on a personal level also. There are plenty of websites dedicated to just this, such as Yoga Trade and Yoga Travel Jobs, that list amazing opportunities regularly, as well as several online groups.

If you have a specific place, country or even venue in mind then do your research and contact venues directly. As with contacting studios, get a feel for what the venues do and their ethos and decide whether this aligns for you and connects to your own teaching style and values. If so, then get in touch with them, letting them know who you are, what you offer, why you love doing what you do and how they will benefit from hiring you. Don't be afraid to express your desire to work there and why you feel so passionately about that, as well as why you're the best match for them. Keep it short and sweet, attach your CV and qualifications and any other links that might be helpful for them to get a feel for you, such as social media. Be sure to initiate further contact such as a phone call to talk about how you could be a part of their team.

If you're more attracted to the idea of running and hosting your own retreats then a good amount of preparation in all aspects is needed, from organizing the logistics and promotion to the planning of the retreat itself and the actual content.

It might be worth considering your following and what they might be ready to commit to retreat wise with you. It would be a good idea to start small, and grow over time, perhaps offering a local weekend retreat to begin with, before investing in a bigger retreat venue, a longer duration and further away, which would have a larger financial and time commitment.

The next section focuses on setting up and running a retreat yourself, looking at it from both an organizational perspective and as a teacher and facilitator, and highlighting some of the things you need to consider.

Running a yoga retreat

JOURNALLING MOMENT

As with other offerings, take some time to consider the following aspects:

- Who is this retreat for?

- Why do you want to offer this retreat and what is the purpose behind it?

- What is it that you want to share on this retreat? This could be the offerings themselves, a theme, a perspective, a deeper look at what you already offer in classes, time with your community, a beautiful place and time in nature. Consider what it is that you feel called to share with your students.

- What type of journey do you want to take students on and what do you want them to walk away with?

- Where is it going to be? What do you need to organize in order to curate this? Is the venue already a retreat venue with everything prepared and you can just rock up and teach or do you need to plan everything from the chef, to the space, props and so on?

- When will the retreat be? It is vital to leave enough lead time to launch the retreat, promote and market it and get bookings in, so probably six months from launching to the actual start date is ideal.

- What other offerings do you want to include, such as extras, excursions, guest facilitators? activities

I hope some of the above questions have already got you thinking about things and pondering some ideas and options. Focusing more on the business side of retreats rather than the creative aspect of what is being offered, let's have a look at the logistics and pricing.

Finding a venue

As mentioned above, when it comes to finding a venue, there are different options open to you. You may wish to approach centres that are well set up and ready to host retreats, so you can arrive free of much of the preparation and focus more on the teaching. Alternatively, you may find a venue, location or villa that you wish to turn into your own retreat space. This will require a little more planning and preparation on your part.

Here are some things to consider:

- Where is the venue? Is it easy to access? Is it very remote (which can have its positives and negatives)?

- How many can it accommodate, both in sleeping but also in the general space, and will that align with the group size you are aiming for?

- Does the venue lend itself well to a retreat? Are there spaces to relax, for people to get some of their own space? Space in nature? Quiet areas to read, contemplate, relax?

- Can the group spaces – dining areas and so on – accommodate your ideal group size?

- Is there a yoga/workshops space? If not, is there a space that can be converted into one and is it open or covered and suitable for all weather and temperatures?

- What is included in the venue? Are there any additional things you'll need to bring that will add to your costs?

Costs and planning

You then need to think about additional planning and costs such as:

- Guest transfers

- Food and chef (and assistant)

- Gifts and giveaways

- Extras – excursions or treatments

Here is a template for planning and pricing your retreat. This is a starting place and you may wish to add in your own elements to make it suitable for your retreat offering.

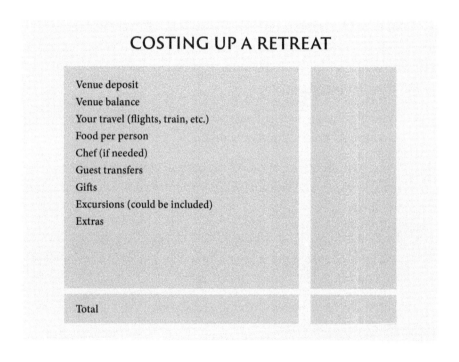

COSTING UP A RETREAT

Venue deposit
Venue balance
Your travel (flights, train, etc.)
Food per person
Chef (if needed)
Guest transfers
Gifts
Excursions (could be included)
Extras

Total

These are starting points for thinking about your retreat and, of course, there is plenty more that could be discussed on this topic. It is recommended that you assist at a retreat or go along and get a feel for how they are run before you offer one yourself. Once it seems like the right time, the clients are in place, you have a plan and are ready to promote it to your audience, then enjoy the process and have an amazing time. Be present and be sure to take time afterwards to note your amazing accomplishments and your learnings for the next one.

Corporate yoga

As we have seen, there are plenty of offering you could make within the yoga industry either as yourself or within a yoga studio. However, your yoga offering does not have to be limited to the 'yoga world' as such, and can be shared in a number of places and ways.

Corporate yoga and wellness has massively boomed around the world and is an incredible way of sharing the magic of yoga and getting people who maybe wouldn't necessarily stumble into a class to begin practising and embarking on their yoga journey. With a greater understanding of the importance of corporate healthcare and wellness, more and more businesses are inviting teachers and practitioners into their spaces to offer yoga, meditation and more. This can be in the form of weekly classes, a one-off course or a workshop.

Corporate yoga can not only be rewarding, fun and expansive as a teacher in many ways, but is also a very lucrative path to go down in regard to work within the yoga business.

If this is the path you feel called to go down, then consider what it is you would like to offer, and who might benefit from this. Approach people you already know and find out if their companies would be open to this offering. Or you could simply cold call or email companies that you feel would benefit from your offerings or you feel drawn to work with. A carefully drafted conscious sales email should be short, sharing what it is that you can offer to help their business and employees and maybe a bit about your experience, your brand, and why you're the right person to support them in improving their health and wellness.

There is usually one person in each corporation who is the go-to contact for this; it might be someone in human resources or someone else, so ask for the right contact to send this information to. Try to make a phone call or engineer an in-person meeting in which you can share more about yourself, what you offer and how you can support their business. Once you feel you have a good understanding of what they would benefit most from and what you can offer them, you can put together a few options of packages bespoke to them, creating professional, branded documents to share the options you want to present, the pricing options and so on.

The pricing structure for corporate offerings can look many ways. Here are some of the options to consider:

- A contract hired as a freelancer.

- Buying into a course or package with various payment structures.

- The company pays 100 per cent of the fees and offers it to their employees. If this is chosen you may decide to have a maximum number of participants per session, and if it goes over perhaps charge an extra fee.

- The company subsidizes the sessions, with students paying a percentage and the company covering the rest of your fee, offering up their space and so on.

- The company provides the time, space and invitation for their employees to join, with the employees paying for the course or sessions themselves.

- The company pays a flat fee to secure you as a teacher with a certain number of students and then employees pay per session when they choose to join.

With some of the above options, you may want to consider what your minimum rate is and if you require a flat starting fee or number of participants signed up in order to confirm the course, class or workshop. You may also have a maximum that you wish to teach in the space, in which case you need participants to sign up in advance and confirm their spaces, and so on. With all of the above options, a contract and terms and conditions should be agreed between you and the company before commencing.

When working in corporate yoga you need to make sure your paperwork is in check, with the right insurance in place, certificates ready to send and possibly an up-to-date first aid certificate (some places will require this and others not, so check if you need to complete this).

When setting up a corporate yoga class or workshop I recommend checking the space you can use beforehand. Make sure it is clean, warm, quiet and preferably private so there aren't many people walking through or past and students can feel comfortable in their practice, not overlooked in any way. You might also want to check the lighting (if you can dim it at all or make it softer) and the temperature (if you can monitor that in any way) and anything else that might affect the experience of the practice. If you require students to have props as part of their practice you may choose to provide these yourself, taking them in each session or maybe seeing if you can store them in the office space, or you may ask students or the company itself to invest in this, which many will happily do if they are committing to a long-term programme.

Opening a yoga space

For some teachers, starting classes and or hiring a venue is not the business path they choose to go down, but instead they wish to set up a venue themselves or perhaps focus their offering elsewhere, such as online. These are equally beautiful and much-needed projects, to create and open a space for transformational work. Opening a physical venue is, of course, a full-time commitment and a long-term investment, so not something that should be jumped into lightly; however, it can be so incredibly rewarding if this is your mission. As with everything, there is so much potential in this realm, but for our purposes we will explore the path of opening up a yoga studio very briefly as a business.

Opening a studio requires a full business plan, and project planning in the same way any big business, studio, fitness studio or gym would. That in itself could be a whole book so please don't take this as your guide to your whole business plan if that is your choice, but instead use it as your starting place. I encourage you to then seek further guidance on business plans, setting up a studio and so on. There are many resources you can gather information from, including books and the internet, and even hiring a business coach or mentor would be a very beneficial step in this path.

I have never personally chosen to set up a studio, as tempting as it has been on many occasions; however, from those I know who have I have seen so much beauty and fulfilment from it, and also the many challenges you can face. Setting up and opening a healing space, whether it be a yoga studio, a retreat centre or anything else, is a big project that requires commitment, dedication, investment, a good understanding of what it is that you're starting and how to run it, open it and so on, and a huge amount of love for what you're doing. From what I have seen from the amazing people I know who have ventured down this path, many of them very successfully, is that it takes a *lot* out of them – their time, their energy and their dedication – and it hasn't always been easy.

Many of the questions and contemplations you were invited to sit with earlier in this chapter are still very much relevant here. Looking at your mission and your business offering as a whole, who you wish to target, what the essence of what you want to offer is and so on – *why* it is that you wish to open a space – is still very much the starting place from which you can begin to explore this idea. Location, size, target audience and so on are all things to consider from the start.

Whether you are choosing to invest and create this yourself, as a group, or to get outside investment, creating a 'start-up deck' is highly recommended. A start-up deck is a presentation that showcases your business and brand idea to potential business partners or investors. It includes your business idea, brand message and vision, mission statement, target audience, team and founders, research, branding (if done), investment required to get going, financial forecasts, timeline of launch and so on, depending on what is relevant to you and your offering.

If you were to look at this business venture as a start-up, what do you need in place in regard to ideas, investment, concepts, research, plans, projections and so on to get this business off the ground? This should be well thought through and prepared, so that if needs be you could present to potential investors or to get a loan. The process of putting this together will be absolutely essential to the early phase of your new project, as well as looking into the business plan, financials and so on. Do your research, stay connected to the vision and embrace this wonderful, immense but ultimately fulfilling path.

Chapter 8

YOUR BUSINESS ADMIN

'Show up with excellence in the big and the small.'

In order to have a successful business, we have to focus on far more than simply the creation, the branding and marketing of it. We also have to put in the work to keep it running on a practical level and maintain the flow of the business. It can be easy at the start to underestimate how much time these aspects can take, as well as how crucial they are to the longevity of your business, and the importance of being business savvy in order to allow it to run with ease, which of course is the dream scenario.

General admin

If you have already been working for a business or in a corporate environment then a lot of this might be very obvious. However, for many of you this might be totally new terrain and so here are some very simple tips to help you stay on top of your daily business admin.

- **Emails:** Keep your email inbox tidy and as clear as possible. If you have enquiries coming in, it is best to try and reply to them as soon as possible, definitely within 24 hours. If you are taking some time offline, let's say you'd prefer to not be looking at emails over the weekend for example, then setting an automated response thanking people for getting in touch and letting them know when to expect a reply from you will be really helpful. This comes across as very professional, can ensure that you keep the potential client, and is a good way of setting boundaries around communication with work. It may even inspire others to not be tied to their emails and feel the need to always respond instantly, even at weekends. Everything you do, even the way you interact via email, can be a way to honour your values and inspire students in some way.

- **Database:** We've already touched on this in regard to building a database and collecting information from potential clients. It's important to have an organized way of collecting this information safely and securely, as of course you have people's personal data. There are many online platforms that can help with this, such as mailchimp, and you can use them to automatically send out newsletters to your students from your database. You may choose to collect the data on your own spreadsheet. I recommend having one main database, and then subgroups if you have specific offerings that certain people are more interested in. For example, if you teach normal classes, but also hold some prenatal offerings, then you can have one mailing list in which you can tell people about the classes on offer, but when you have a new prenatal course starting or a special promotion aimed at this demographic, a separate group already exists for this purpose and you can easily 'target' them with your marketing.

- **Contracts:** You may need to write up contracts, or sign contracts, as part of your business. If you are going into a partnership with anyone, whether that be a business partner, venue, supplier or even sometimes clients, writing a contract can lay a solid foundation and boundaries for both parties in this business relationship. There are many contract templates to be found online, or if you feel you need more professional advice then seek the support of a lawyer, especially if the contract is for a bigger business partnership or commitment.

- **Health forms:** Whether you have a studio, are teaching in person or via online classes, or are running retreats, asking for a health form to be completed by your clients is essential. On your health form you can collect their personal information and contact details, but also gather essential health information that will allow you to hold space for them better in your offerings and make sure you can support them and any illness or injuries they may have. It can be very helpful to get these in advance in case you need to ask more questions, or perhaps even do some research if they are suffering with something you are unsure of and need to look into more. Health forms can also be the perfect opportunity to gather information such as what someone is looking to get from working with you, maybe what their hopes are and so on, which can of course also help in your offering depending on what that is. Another way of using health forms can be as a track for a student's progress, depending on how personally you are working with them. This is particularly helpful for private tuition, as this personal development and growth can be nice to monitor and track and be offered back as a reflection every few months maybe, for both you as a facilitator and the student on their journey. You may want to add other conditions into your health forms, and be sure they are signed and dated by the clients.

- **Terms and conditions:** These are any terms and conditions you may want to put in place and agree on in regard to your offering. For example, if you are offering a payment structure, it may be that you need them to sign the agreement on this and when the payments are due. You may choose to include cancellation policies, what is and isn't included in the offering and so on. This is an opportunity to set clear boundaries and expectations on both sides for a clean and clear working relationship. Again, many examples of these can be found online as a starting place to build your own, depending of course on your business and what it is that you're offering.

Finances

When it comes to finances and your accounts, keeping them in order and staying on top of it all is vital. It can be easy at the beginning, especially if you're not super busy at first, to be a little more relaxed with this, but getting into the rhythm of being organized and having a system in place from the start will be incredibly beneficial as you grow. Our attitude towards money and earning can often have some limiting beliefs or emotional energy behind it. I've found that the more disciplined we are in how we interact with money, including simply being on top of paying bills, the way we receive money and are aware of the flow and exchange can in itself develop a very healthy attitude to money and therefore a healthy abundance in our life.

Try to implement an accounts system, whether that be a simple Excel spreadsheet or an online system that tracks all of your incomings and outgoings. There are many ways you can break this down, monthly, quarterly, and so on, and into categories that work for you. There are many systems online that you can use if this is something you don't have much experience with. Many of these systems can also be used for online invoicing. Alternatively, you can create your own template to send out to clients via email.

Whether you decide to register as a company or a sole trader, be sure to put aside the tax that will be payable, and I recommend keeping a little bit kept aside for any miscellaneous expenses that could come along. You may choose to use an accountant, which of course can be incredibly helpful, but isn't essential. I do, however, suggest that you get some advice to make sure that you're following all of the financial and government requirements that are needed for your type of business.

Licences and insurance

It is essential to get fully insured with anything that you decide to offer. As a freelancer, it is your responsibility to do this in order to be covered, and all studios, corporates and so on will ask for your insurance certificates before you begin working with them. There are several companies that offer this, and many that are specifically for the wellness industry, so do some research to find the one that works best for you. Many will have some options for additional coverage, so decide what you personally need based on what and where you're planning on teaching.

Some licences may also need to be acquired, such as a music licence if you decide to play your own music in your classes as these are considered public use. In the UK, you need to get a music licence to play music publicly from PPL PRS. There are some websites that provide music that is free to play so you can also look for these options. This is also the case if you are using any music for online content, so again be sure to check your usage rights before using any artists' material for your work.

If you choose to teach in certain parks or public areas, you may need to apply for a licence. In London, for example, you need to get a specific licence to teach in most parks, so be sure to check beforehand.

Governing bodies

The yoga industry is technically an unregulated industry still; however, there are many governing bodies that are passionate about establishing a set standard and regulations across the board. As of yet, it is not a necessity to be connected to any of these, although there are definitely benefits to doing so, and in supporting them in making sure that the overall standard of training, teaching and support for teachers is kept high. To find out more about this and what they can offer you, check out Yoga Alliance Professionals for the UK governing body. There are other international governing bodies, such as Yoga Alliance US, that have been established a while, so it could be worth reading into the options to find one that resonates best with you and considering what they can offer you as a yoga professional.

— Chapter 9 —

BUILDING YOUR
WEBSITE

'Put the work in and then let it work.'

Although a website is not necessarily an essential requirement for any business, having an online presence is extremely helpful in today's climate, especially with the emphasis on online searching, social media and so on. A website allows you and your business to have a platform to which you can direct people, that simply explains who you are, what you do and anything else you wish to offer online, which will vary person to person. Of course, a website can be far more than that, and in these times many people choose to have a business that runs predominantly online with online courses, programmes and classes. The important thing is to create and design a website that suits you, your brand and the function and purpose for which you need it.

As much as a website can be a daunting project for some to consider, it really doesn't have to be, and can actually be simple and easy to set up. With many options for how to go about building one, it can be done in a way that isn't too financially demanding.

Hiring a website designer vs. building your own website

When considering your website there are of course many ways you can look at it. If you have the funds, then hiring a professional to support you with the design and build is a wonderful option. With professional support you'll not only be guided through the entire process, but they'll also be able to share some great tips based on their experience and knowledge. They'll know what works well for you and your needs, how to create an attractive website design, and have some insider tips on boosting your search engine optimization (more on this later).

In regard to support, you can work with anyone from a website development business, to a freelancer, to a student who might want to do a trade with you. As with working with a designer or anyone else who can support you with your business, there are many ways in which you can get support that aren"t always necessarily a financial trade, but could be an exchange of yoga lessons for website support for example. Feel into what investment you are comfortable with at this moment, knowing it really is an investment. Work with what is possible now, and if investing more into this is something you want to move towards then that could be seen as a good financial target perhaps, to then maybe rebuild or get support in the future.

The exciting part about websites, unlike many years ago, is that it is now absolutely possible to build a great one yourself using the many online platforms designed for exactly this. You don't need to be a designer, a coder or have a lot of funds to invest in it in order to have a beautiful, clean, sleek and functional website. In fact, a lot of really wonderful websites I come across have been built on these platforms with very little cost and not only look great but work perfectly for what they are needed for. So as always, decide what feels right for you in regard to cost and honour that, then see what your options are.

Whichever path you take, whether working with a professional or building the website yourself, it's important to be really clear on exactly what it is you want and need from your website, otherwise it can be quite a challenge to create. Some guidance and a clear vision from you will help the process, and give you a better chance of getting what you really want out of it.

Whether working with an external web designer, or if building it yourself, write a brief (a description of what you want and need from your website). Go into as much detail as possible. Having this clarity before you get started can make the process much quicker, and more enjoyable. I personally love building websites as I see it as a creative outlet and another way of communicating with my audience, capturing people, and expressing and sharing what I do. So, if the idea of building a website is daunting in any way, I invite you to try and shift the perspective, and make it a creative and exciting new avenue to express yourself, your brand and share what you do with the world.

If you've decided to outsource your website build, hire a professional or trade with someone to build your website for you, then asking friends, family and peers for recommendations is always a great starting place.

Ask the person for some examples of their work, their costs, the timeline in which they can complete it and also what the ongoing support looks like. This is important because as you grow as a business it's likely you'll want – and need – to make updates to your website to either add things in, edit things, update images or text and so on. You may choose to start to offer an online course, or your schedule will change –whatever it is, it's important to know if this is something you can update yourself or if they'll need to do it for you and if so what that looks like. It will depend on how they've built it, what the back end of your website is like, and if you can access that, so make sure it's super clear before you get going. You may also want to find out what other technical support they can give you, especially if you're looking to have things like online payments available and links to newsletter sign-ups, so that it can all be seamless.

Website inspiration

Before you begin, take some time to feel inspired. Do some research and decide what you actually like and don't like. I remember the first time I really thought about building my first website. I had no idea what I wanted or where to begin and someone asked me to go and create a list of websites I liked. I was invited to browse through websites similar to what I was looking to create and note down what I liked about them and what I really didn't like. I was so surprised at what I got from this exercise. In reality, I hadn't considered how different websites were before that moment, not only in they looked, but the navigation of them and the feel of them. It can be pretty eye-opening and actually amazing to think about how much we are online and looking at websites, but don't necessarily pay much attention to the style, functionality and so on, even though we are probably drawn to a site and it captures us and keeps our attention. We can sometimes just take that all for granted.

With that being said, I highly recommend doing just that. Go ahead and check out a load of websites and start to get inspired. Maybe look at teachers you like, people you follow or are inspired by, or just anyone you come across. They might be in yoga and be perhaps someone who does something similar to you or a teacher you respect, and they might not. It doesn't have to be a website that would be like yours or a business like yours, it's more about the look and the functionality of it, so the content doesn't matter so much (but of course can be helpful to see the variety of ways it can be done).

WEBSITE INSPIRATION

Here are some things to bear in mind when you're browsing websites:

- What do you like and not like?

- What attracts your eye and what makes you lose interest?

- How does the website look when you first open it? Is there a landing page? Does it have a pop-up promotion/sign up? Are you confronted with a big beautiful photo first or a title or a logo or a video? Or something else?

- How does the website 'move' (how does it scroll)? Is the whole website on one big page that continuously scrolls down, or is it on many pages? Is it easy for you to navigate and obvious to find what you are looking for?

- Is there a menu? If so, where is it?

- What does the home page look like?

- Where is the website directing you to? Does it have a call to action that takes you to a programme, product sale or to get in touch with them?

- Is it clear and obvious what it offers?

- Can you get the information you want easily?

- Is it showing you obvious points of interest such as a 'selling point', a call to action, a sign-up?

- What are the images like?

- What is the general design like?

With all of these elements to consider, write down what you notice and, more importantly, what you like about it and what doesn't really resonate as well for you. As you are going through the websites, also note what you might want on your website; for example, you might really like the pages the person had, or the way they used images. You might also take note of the language used, the way in which they communicate and so on.

For the following exercise, take some time to sit quietly and reflect. You'll want at least 15 minutes for this and will need your notebook.

JOURNALLING MOMENT

Take a moment to notice your experience on the website. Sit and feel into your body and then write about the following:

- How did the website make you feel?

- Was it easy to use? Inspiring? Pretty?

- Did it make you want to know more?

- Did it stir anything in you and do you feel called to work with this person?

- Did anything feel jarring for you?

All of these things can really help you figure out what will be best for your website, whether it's you doing it yourself or someone else.

Building your own website

If you've decided to build your website yourself then here are a few of the popular website build platforms I would recommend (and of course there are many others that are also excellent, this is just a selection I am familiar with at this time):

- Squarespace

- Wix

- Zyro

- WordPress

- Weebly.

These all vary in regard to the templates offered, the cost, the ease and speed at which you can build and create on them, how user-friendly and intuitive they are as well as what is available on them. Check out a few, do some research and have a read of what they offer. They can really vary, but essentially all have their pros and cons so go with the one that offers most of what you want and has the templates you are most drawn to.

The templates are the 'base' from which you can build your website yourself. So, whereas when you hire someone to build a website for you they might use code to build a unique backend for your site, when you use a website-building platform that has templates, this has already been done for you, so no coding or tech savvy skills are needed. You can get a beautiful clean template for a website that allows you to go in and edit and change it to make it look and flow the way you want. It really can be that easy. All of these platforms have great user-friendly tools, little prompts to help you along the way, tutorials, videos and so on. You can change as little or as much of the template as you want (the majority of the time).

When looking at templates, it's best to opt for one that flows in a way that you like. So, notice the navigation of the website, the way the pages are, the scrolling, the general layout and the overall design and feel of the website. Try not to get too caught up in the details or images as these will all change with your own when you start to work on the design. Everything, from the colours, the fonts, the images, the placement of text and more, can be edited, so try not to focus too much on that, unless you love it how it is, in which case brilliant, even less for you to change.

If you love the template as it is, it can be as easy as switching the images for your own, adding your logo in, linking it up to your domain and writing in your own text and there you have it, your website! Easy right!? It really can be. I've built websites in a day. When it comes to websites, simplicity is key. First and foremost, you want your students to be able to see what you do clearly, who you are, get the information they need easily, navigate the site easily and get a sense of you and your brand through it. This doesn't take much, so don't over complicate it or get caught up in putting too much in or you may lose customers along the way.

For example, if you're wanting to promote and share an online yoga course, make that super obvious from the beginning. Have it on your main page. Let it be an easy click through for more information, or to book rather than having it hidden on some other page at the bottom, where they need to click on three things to get to what they want. What they need to know is what is the course? Where is it? How much is it? What will they get from it? And how do they sign up?

WEBSITE TOP TIPS

Here are some top things to consider when building your website:

- Keep your navigation simple. This means keeping the structure of the website, the pages, simple.

- Have an obvious menu and keep it short. People have very short attention when opening a new website so grab your perfect audience quickly by showing them you are who they're looking for.

- Be clear and show what your focus is from the main page.

- Always consider your audience.

- Have calls to action – for example 'Available for 24 hours only' or 'Secure your space now'.

- Be you and stay on brand throughout. This includes images, using your logo, the colours of the brand, and the copy.

- Use high resolution images.

- Make sure your website is mobile friendly.

- Have a clean and clear homepage. Try to avoid clutter or too much information and text.

COMMON MISTAKES

Here are some common website pitfalls made when building your own website that you should be aware of:

- Too much – too many images, too much text, too much going on in general that takes away from the key message.

- Not enough – it doesn't actually give enough information or offer what people are looking for.

- Unclear navigation – it's not obvious where to click or how to move around, and people get lost in it, unable to access what they need.

- Design – if the design isn"t great, for example the images don't fit well, it doesn't match the design and look of the brand all together.

- Missing the audience – you haven't designed the website with your target audience in mind.

Domain name

In order to have a live website you need a domain name. This is the actual unique url for your website (www.yourwebsitename…). It may end in .com or .co.uk or something else. There are many places you can buy your domain name online, a few popular places being:

- www.godaddy.com

- www.123-reg.co.uk

- www.bluehost.com

- www.domain.com

- www.namecheap.com

…and more. There are many to choose from, each with different things on offer so do some research to find the one that works best for you. With some of these you may want to check if they include emails, and if so, how many email addresses are linked to the website and how many would you need. Some of the actual website-building platforms have a service that allows you to buy the domain name through them directly, as well as the email addresses, and it can be easier to have it all in one place. It's a very personal choice so check some options to find the one that feels best for you.

If you decide to go with a different domain name registration company then linking this to your website-building platform is usually very easy. There is most likely a guide or tutorial on how to do this within your website-building system. Once it is redirected, it can take just a few hours to be active.

When it comes to choosing your domain name, you will most likely be opting for your brand name. If you did your research when working on the branding initially, you will have chosen a unique name, or at least unique for your area or country so that people can find you more easily. If this is the case then it's probable that your desired domain name is available. If for any reason it isn't, then your options are to choose a different variation, meaning going for the .co.uk instead of the .com, or perhaps adding something on the name itself, for example adding yoga to the end of the name, or wellness, if that feels supportive of your brand and search-ability. If this still doesn't fit well, then it may be that it has to change slightly. For some people, using their actual personal name instead of their brand name is more optimal, if they know that the business will be staying under their personal name long term. This can be helpful when searching for the website if people will more commonly search for your name instead of the brand. But, ideally, you'll want people to be able to find you through searching both.

Search engine optimization (SEO)

Search engine optimization, known as SEO, is the way in which your website is searched and found online through search engines, such as google or yahoo. A website's SEO is what helps it be searched for more easily and have a more optimal result in an online search. For example, when someone searches yoga in your local area on google, you'll ideally want to be at the top of the results list. This is the purpose of SEO. It is therefore pretty important when it comes to a website as it is what allows new people to find you online. It is, of course, not the only way, there are other little hacks, as well as promoting yourself through other avenues and then directing your audience to your website. But, to attract new online clients it is pretty important. There are many ways to increase your SEO, and it changes regularly. A professional website builder will be very focused on this and this can be a benefit of using a professional; however, there are ways to improve this yourself too. Each website-building platform will also have tips and tutorials to help you, and some even have a function that actually scans your website and shows you things to change to help increase your SEO.

TOP TIPS TO BOOSTING YOUR SEO

- Use keywords in your copy. Keywords are words that people might search for to find you. You'll want to make sure that these are written in your titles and main copy so that they can be picked up by search engines. However, don't overdo it. Make your website for your audience, not for a search engine.

- Publish high-quality content.

- Add titles to your images.

- Use effective header tags and titles to help break up big chunks of content and help search engines to identify your page and content compatibility.

- Use different types of high-quality media – clear images, maybe adding videos to bring a page to life. Make sure these are optimized by tagging them and giving them titles.

- Blogging. Having an active blog that is updated regularly can help with this.

- Make sure your website is mobile friendly. Many website-building platforms will have a tool to assist with this and as the majority of users these days search on their mobile it is essential to make this clean.

Website content

When it comes to your website, the most important aspect is the actual content. Once you get people landing on your page, it's the content that they've come for, and that will keep them and, we hope, convert them into clients and new students.

Writing the copy for your website can sometimes seem like an arduous job, but once again, simplicity really is key. You have already done so much in creating your brand, your mission statement, your offerings, so you really have all the material you need for this content. It's now a case of simply picking out the key elements that need to be shared on your website, and making it clear, succinct and enticing. Make sure the language you use feels authentic to you and your business and speaks to your ideal client, the yogi avatar.

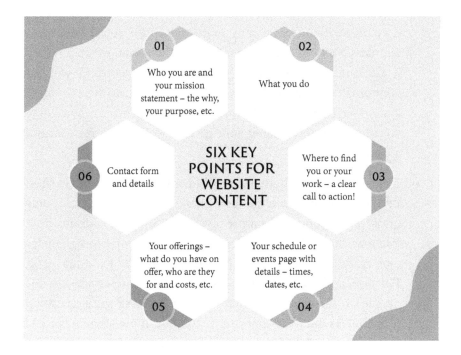

There are some additional things you may wish to include. These are a few ideas that can add a little something extra to your website, might make you stand out more, help people connect with you and really feel you and your brand:

- **Introduction video:** This can be pretty daunting to do, but it is the best way for people to get a feel for you straightaway. This could be a simple video about your business, you and your offerings.

- **Newsletter sign up and pop-up promotional boxes:** These are the boxes that show up when you've been on a website after a few seconds and can be a great way to get someone's details and sign them up to your newsletter, or let them know about a promotion, upcoming course and so on. Keep them simple and I recommend only having one otherwise it can start to overwhelm the client and lose them.

- **Booking systems and ecommerce:** There are many ways to link up an automatic booking and payment system to your website. Maybe website-building platforms have third-party companies they link with automatically to do this and if you're wanting a seamless booking and payment method this is an easy way to do it. You can then implement a payment flow that works for you and is automated. Some of these will take a fee for using their payment system so it's important to consider this percentage when doing your finances and pricing your classes, workshops, retreats and so on.

- **Downloads:** Offering a free download of something, such as a short film of a yoga practice, can be a great way for people to not only get a feel for you, but be more invested in you and your business. You may choose to do this as a way of getting people to sign up for your newsletter for example. We are all s familiar with this tactic, I'm sure, and it can feel a bit 'salesy' at times; however, only the people who are genuinely interested in your work will sign up and it then gives them an opportunity to know more about what you do, so in the end it's a great tool to link you with your ideal clients.

Linking it all together

- Make sure you connect your database and newsletter to your website, so that through your sign-up you're not missing out on any potential new clients.

- Set up google analytics to your website.

- Link any social media you are using so people can follow you and connect with you.

There is of course so much more that can be covered when it comes to websites, but hopefully these main points have got you going and given you enough to create, build and launch the perfect website for your business. Remember to keep it clear and simple. Keep checking in with your branding and your mission statement and stay consistent in your message, communication and ethos, as well as your look and feel. Give your website creation some love, energy and time, don't rush the process, but enjoy it and let it be another form of expressing your business with the world. If you're posting regularly on there, for example writing a blog, then be consistent and make sure you stay on top of it, updating it regularly. Lastly, be patient with it. It can take some time for a website to gain some traction, but the more you stay working on it, seeing ways to optimize it, linking it with your social media or directing people there, the more it will grow and attract new clients.

Website analytics

In the same way you should check the performance of your social media, you should also regularly check your website data and analytics. This will give you a better overview of traffic to your website, traffic to each page, the way in which people interact with your website and so on. It can also show you where people are being directed to your website from, which can give you a great understanding of where to direct your energy. For example, if you notice that the majority of traffic is to a particular page, coming directly from your Instagram account, then you can maybe put more time and energy into generating and utilizing Instagram content. It might also show you where you are not getting the results you wish. If you are not getting much traffic to your website from search engines such as google, then it might be worth investing more time on your SEO and looking at ways to increase your ranking on search pages.

Your analytics will continue to change, with daily information available if you choose to check it, so do make this a regular part of maintaining your business, and update your website based on this feedback.

If you have a low performing page, or low click through to sales/booking rate, then take the time to see how you can update the page, move things around, change the wording and so on to get the desired results.

Chapter 10

BUSINESS DEVELOPMENT

'Who are you becoming?
And again? And again? And again?'

Business plan

In this book, we have gone into detail about writing mission statements, identifying ideal clients, deciding on branding and so on. We have looked at various ways to work in the yoga industry, various offerings and ways to go about generating these. Depending on what your business model is, you may or may not want or even need a business plan, in the more traditional sense. Of course, every business has a business plan, meaning even the freelancers who 'wing it' have a direction and steps they can see themselves taking, even if it isn't too far ahead. Most businesses, however, will have more of a forward trajectory that they are moving towards, and elements of the business they have thought through, essentially to guarantee that the business actually works, is functioning and profitable, and there is a market for it. If in the initial stages of setting up a business there are some obvious fundamental problems in the business plan, then you already have something to address before developing your brand and doing any promotional work. This level of detail may not apply to everyone. For example, if you're choosing to teach in studios then a business plan probably isn't necessary. However, if you want to scale up your business in any way, whether that be opening a studio, building a bigger brand, building a corporate business or retreating company, then this additional piece is a must. If you ever wish to approach business partners or investors, then a business plan will be required as a way of showing future plans and ideas, and that these have been through and researched, and essentially will work.

We won't be going into depth in this, as really it depends greatly on the business idea itself; however, we have produced a rough guideline or a basic starting place for a business plan. You may choose to go into much more detail or find information elsewhere for guidance on financial forecasting and so on, if that feels needed.

Whatever your yoga business is, I recommend completing the exercise below as a way of pulling together all you have worked on so far in this book, and elsewhere, into one place, as well as being good practice for maintaining a high standard of business practice.

EXERCISE

Take a moment to go back over all the notes you have made and review them. Check that they all still resonate and then you can begin to fill in the gaps in the chart below. You may want to do it here, or create your own that you can print off and work with.

Complete the business plan as follows in a succinct way, bringing together all the information you have gathered and ideas you have created so far.

Brand description: What?
An introduction to the business concept and basic model of the business.

Core message: Why?
This is the 'why' around your business. Why do you feel called to do this? What is your mission statement, your purpose, your passion and your core values as a business?

Clients: Who?
A description of who your target audience are (referred to in

previous chapters as your yogi avatar). What do they need your services for and what do they desire?

Client challenge: Why?
Why do they need you? What are the main challenges or pain points your dream client or students face?

Your offering: How?
What is it that you can offer to help with your clients' challenges and alleviate a problem they may have? Why would they need your services and how can you help with this?

Revenue stream: How much?
These are your revenue goals, how much you intend on having as an income weekly, monthly or yearly. What is your desired salary, and how do you hope to reach this goal? Maybe break down how much each offering is and what quantity or frequency you must reach in order to succeed in fulfilling this desired outcome.

Pricing: How much?
Based on research, the local market and your desired financial goals, how much will you be charging for your classes, packages or offerings?

Go to market: Where?
Where do you plan on offering your work and how do you plan promoting, generating sales or bookings and marketing your business and offerings?

Investment required: How much?
Do you require a certain amount to get your business started and to make it a success? If so, how much is this and where are your potential investments coming from?

Business growth: How?
How do you see your business developing and growing over time? Do you have any ideas for future visions and expansions or offerings?

> **Timeline: When?**
> Create a rough timeline of what you see happening when in the stages of business development and your first few years running.

Business development

In order to keep the flow of abundance in your business, not only financially but also in regard to work flow, students, bookings, collaborations, new projects and so on, it is important to continuously dedicate time to your business development and planning. This can be practised in many ways, but here are a few ideas to inspire you:

- **Yearly planning:** Mapping out your whole year is essential for a business. When you become financially reliant on your own business income, then it is vital not only to plan ahead, but also to know you will have consistent work coming in and a regular salary. If for any reason this is not consistent, then this should be something you have pre-planned for and taken into consideration in regard to payments, savings and spending.

    Planning your year ahead also allows you to plan much needed, and deserved, time off and holidays to rest and recharge. When we start out with our own business this is often forgotten, which can lead to burnout, so make sure you plan in your time off so that you can continue to show up full of energy and inspired to do what you do. When putting together your yearly plan you want to be able to identify long-term commitments, shorter projects, and work that will be more ad hoc. Write down your ideal scenario, what these will need regarding time commitments and what the income and outgoings are for each. Some things might be quicker to develop, such as booking in new private clients. However, bigger workshops, corporate courses and retreats may need a much longer lead time for both planning, securing venues and, of course, promotion.

    It can be fun when you do this to look at what you'd love to have achieved by the end of the year. This can be financially, and also in

BUSINESS PLAN

Date: _____

**MY BRAND
DESCRIPTION**

CLIENTS

CORE MESSAGE

BUSINESS GROWTH

CLIENT CHALLENGE

TIMELINE

○

○

○

YOUR OFFERING

INVESTMENT

**REVENUE STREAM
AND PRICING**

GO TO MARKET

regard to your heart's desire and what you'd love to have worked on in the year ahead, and where you envision your business to be in a year's time. You can then work backwards, looking at the steps needed to get there in that time, breaking it down into monthly or quarterly goals.

- **A monthly plan:** This would include your classes and events that are coming up, what you need to focus on and prepare, what needs to be promoted and marketed and where time is required to do some admin, for example update your website or actively work on creating exciting social media content. Look at what areas of your business need love and some of your time, and what your desired outcome is in a month's time. What do you wish to see change, grow, develop or be completed?

- **Goals:** You may choose to have a yearly, monthly or weekly goal-setting session. I like to do this at the start of each month and then again every Monday morning as a way to get my week going and set clear intentions for the month or week ahead. This might include specific goals in regard to classes, clients and finances. It could be anything from, 'By the end of December I have secured three new weekly private clients' to, 'I have increased my monthly income to £3000 by securing one more corporate client'.

The more specific, detailed and clear you are with your goals the better. It is often encouraged to write them in positive language and in the present tense and to identify a specific time frame. Taking the time to write these targets out not only sets a clear intention, but helps you focus and whether consciously or subconsciously work towards them by the end of the year, month or week. If you have a big goal in mind, then take the time to focus on it daily, maybe even placing your goal somewhere you can read it every day as a reminder to help generate energy and abundance around it. I have found this to be an incredibly effective way of keeping me on track, never losing sight of the bigger picture and creating the business I desire.

Chapter 13

CONCLUSION

'Trust every step of the journey.'

As you've made your way through this book you've been on a journey. A journey to birthing your dream business, which includes stepping into your purpose and following a conscious career path, as well as a journey of self-discovery. These two points go hand in hand within this industry as we walk the talk, authentically embody who we are and what we then choose to share. This is a starting place, a stepping stone to a new beginning for you and your business, and it is a path that is ever moving, changing and unfolding.

I hope that within these pages you have found some insight, tools, tips and inner wisdom to guide you to your next phase. This book is the foundation for stepping into your yoga business, and ultimately there are many options that still lie ahead for you on this path.

Know that many of the exercises and ideas here can serve you throughout your career, and you may choose to revisit them as you change and reassess the path you are taking. You may come back to this book with each evolutionary phase of your business, when you feel you are ready for a new direction in your career, whether that be stepping into a new business model, opening a studio, setting up a teacher training or anything else that might come from your experience and aspirations moving forwards.

Whatever you choose to do, stay connected to your source, your intuition and deeper purpose and mission. Remember the sky view in both your mind and heart and let that guide you as you go. Listen to your inner wisdom, as well as learning from each experience. It is important that we maintain standards in the yoga industry, that we keep the bar high and always offer the absolute best we can. With this in mind, commit to maintaining your own high standards, to keep learning and developing in your own teaching and seeking out further education and training that can support you as you grow.

I encourage you to seek out teachers and trainings that inspire you and can continue to set your soul alight. This is so important, to keep you not only evolving in your business and staying on top of new information, but also remaining passionate about what you do and continuing to challenge yourself and grow.

As you step up in the way that you show up in the yoga industry and your business, you encourage others to step up with you. You can influence and inspire those around you, as well as make way for others to follow in your path sharing this transformative work.

Enjoy each and every step and embrace all that comes your way on this journey.

INDEX